SURVIVAL 2 —

A Manual
of
Primitive
Outdoor
Skills

Compiled by
Richard L. Jamison

International Standard Book Number
0-88290-203-2

Library of Congress Catalog Card Number
82-81292

Horizon Publishers Catalog and Order Number
4031

Fourth Printing, February 1984

Cover photo and design by Richard Jamison

About The Authors

Ron "Gus" Gustaveson has studied primitive skills for over twenty years. His interest in archaeology and ethnology has prompted his experimentation with various methods of the skills he has learned. His willingness to share his knowledge adds greatly to the annual Woodsmoke Rendezvous workshop. Gus is a contributing author for *Woodsmoke Journal* and a conscientious instructor.

Cecil Hamilton has been conducting training classes in outdoor skills for many years, both privately and through the community college in Arkansas City, Kansas. He is a published author of articles on outdoor subjects and has been a regular contributor to *Woodsmoke Journal.* Cecil is expert in both wild plant identification and use and herbal medicine, and is also an accomplished craftsman in primitive skills.

Paul Hellweg teaches primitive life styles and lithics (stone working) for the Leisure Studies program at California State University in Northridge. An expert climber and free-lance writer, Paul has written a walking tour guide for rock climbers in the Los Angeles area titled *Stony Point Guide.*

Linda Jamison has taught classes in wild plant identification at the University of Southern Colorado, University of Colorado, El Paso Community College in Colorado Springs, and to many clubs and organizations. She is the managing editor of *Woodsmoke Journal* and a published free-lance writer.

Richard Jamison is a noted outdoor photographer and writer. He has produced a series of ten outdoor educational films which are used in schools throughout the nation and by other instructors. Richard received national recognition for his skill in primitive craftsmanship and knowledge of aboriginal skills when he worked as technical advisor and set designer on the film "Windwalker." He is the director of Anasazi Expeditions and editor and publisher of *Woodsmoke Journal.*

Larry Dean Olsen, author of the best-selling book *Outdoor Survival Skills,* originated the award-winning "480" 30-day survival trek at Brigham Young University. He has been a pioneer in instigating primitive survival courses as an effective rehabilitation program in the United States. Larry has lectured and taught primitive survival throughout the nation. He is currently involved in a civil defense program based in California.

Jim Riggs conducts aboriginal life style expeditions for the Malheur and Wallowa field stations in Oregon. He is an accomplished artist and illustrator, and the author of *Blue Mountain Buckskin,* an authoritative book on the Indian brain tanning method of making buckskin. Jim majored in anthropology at Oregon State University and, as a result of his superb craftsmanship and his knowledge of the primitive life style of the early Great Basin people, has been asked to contribute his work to the Oregon High Desert Museum.

Mack Smith has personally led more than a thousand people across more than 5,000 miles of some of the roughest deserts in the world during the last fifteen years. Mack specializes in programs that emphasize improved mental attitude and personal development. In addition to his involvement in the outdoors and as an expedition leader, Mack is a school teacher and lecturer.

Larry Wells is director of Expedition Outreach, a program of wilderness rehabilitation. Larry has worked as a drug abuse counselor and probation and parole officer for the state of Idaho in addition to conducting many trips and training sessions for different agencies in Idaho, Nevada, Utah, Arizona and New Mexico. Larry is author of *A Guide to Wilderness Therapy Programs* and a survival manual entitled *You Can Stay Alive,* as well as other articles dealing with outdoor skills.

Ernest Wilkinson is a nationally renowned outdoor photographer, writer and lecturer. He was principal photographer for the film *Cougar Country* which featured his own mountain lion Tabby. Ernest and his wife, Margaret, raise many wild animals such as cougars, badgers, wolves, coyotes and bobcats. He is an expert guide and survival instructor, and has worked as a government trapper and taxidermist for many years in the San Luis valley of Colorado.

Gary Wisdom is a member of the U.S. Navy Survival Team. His vast experience of survival in many parts of the world and in varied conditions makes his knowledge indispensible. Gary plays an important part in testing new, as well as old, survival techniques for effectiveness under stress situations. This experience gives him valuable insight into the psychological as well as physical conditioning needed in emergency situations.

Contents

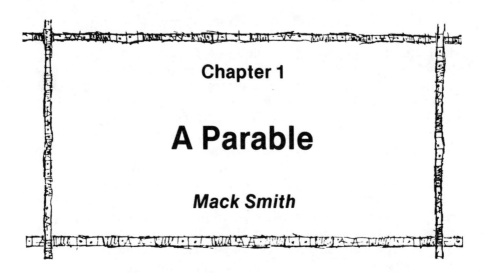

Chapter 1

A Parable

Mack Smith

Early one morning I was nearly to the top of Mt. Ellen, almost 12,000 feet above the surrounding deserts. The air was cold and as clear as the water I had drunk earlier from the spring below. The sun rose in a golden flare over the LaSalle Mountains on the Colorado border, flooding the land with a light that intensified its multiple hues of reds and golds. The land that had seemed so flat, grey, and featureless now was revealed by the slanting light to be a land thrust up and twisted by the forces beneath it, cut and ravaged by the inexorable movement of water, and smoothed and rounded by the endless polishing of windborne sand.

I continued climbing up these broken bones of the world that had pushed themselves through the covering of trees almost 2,000 feet lower, and shortly reached the top. Up here the wind ruled, sucking the heat of the sun away from my body as I turned. It didn't blow, swirl, or gust; it just moved with a steady unending and irresistible pressure over these small obstacles in its path.

As I turned, I realized that nearly one-fourth of the state of Utah was spread out below me. In the north was the somber line of the Roan Cliffs, northwest was the eroded dome of the San Rafael Swell and the beginnings of the red and white rounded thousand-foot sandstone ridge of the Waterpocket Fold. That carried my eyes in a majestic sweep past the twin blue peaks of Thousand Lake and Boulder Mountain, the seventy-mile line of Straight Cliffs and the Kaparowits Plateau to end at the hulking blue dome of Navajo Mountain to the south of the Arizona border. Turning again to the east, the convolutions of deserts and canyons surrounding the Colorado, Green and Dirty Devil rivers stood out in bold relief.

As the immense panorama poured in upon my senses, I felt my spirit beginning to swell. As I looked about me again, I could see below in the open meadows the black forms of the buffalo, and I could feel their pleasure in the new warmth of the sun on their shaggy coats. I heard a sharp, clear cry and looking up and out saw the eagle, sunlight glancing from his golden wings, soaring on the great wave of wind rising over the mountain. I could feel his control and strength as he twisted his wingtips and moved on the invisible currents that throbbed against my body.

The power of the occasion began to fill my heart until I felt I was overflowing my body and beginning to drift free from the earth. I began to see more clearly the intertwining of all things; the badger digging in a new gopher hole, the antelope flashing over a sandy ridge and a coyote moving out of their path. The kangaroo rat avoiding the rattlesnake sunning himself, the patches of green indicating the presence of water in a land of reds and golds.

My senses were overcome by all that I saw and felt, and there was a great blending of everything around me.

Then it seemed as if my vision cleared and I felt in another place of light. The Great Spirit was speaking to many spirits. He said, "You have all learned and progressed as much as possible in this place. If you stay longer, you will become less."

He took Gaia by the hand and asked if she would be the mother earth for all. She said nothing, but smiled and nodded her willingness.

The spirits of the plants and animals were lovely and simple, and they desired only to grow, live, and be. They were placed and became one with the earth. And they were happy and derived much pleasure from their existence.

Then the Great Spirit called the spirits of the people together. "You are a special problem," he said. "You have much intelligence, but you have not learned to use it wisely. You have the ability and, therefore, the right to make decisions for yourself, but sometimes you do not make good decisions. You have much freedom here, but you do not appreciate that freedom.

"Therefore, when you go to earth you will have many limitations. Your only freedom will be freedom of choice. You will no longer fly as the birds, or run as the antelope, or see as the eagle, or swim as the salmon, or be as strong as the bear. Because of these limitations you will have to use your intelligence to discover how to overcome them. From this you will learn the value of freedom, challenges, and correct decisions. You must also watch the other creatures and the earth and learn from them, and learn how we are bound together as if in the web of a great spider. Go now my children, and learn and grow."

And then I left that bright, warm, happy place and I saw the earth floating like a blue and white bubble in a dark sea.

I watched the many creatures living together with the earth and saw broken places in the pattern, and I saw people there. Some were making good decisions and repairing the pattern, and some were not. Some were learning, and some were hindering others from learning. Some were living free, and some were preventing others from living free. And some didn't care.

I saw a young man cut down a tree, laughing as it fell. He walked away, proud of his strength, and I felt sad for him and the tree.

I looked again and saw an old man lovingly select a tree and, with a prayer of thanks in his heart, he carefully cut it down. I saw him make many useful things from the wood with his own hands, treasuring the feel of the wood as his creations took shape.

I gradually became aware that I was still on the mountain and, after absorbing more of the surroundings with my whole soul, I turned and walked back down to the world of men.

Wilderness

Way out there,
Not caring where,
Wolf,
Coyote
Beckon me
With promises of dreams
And miles and miles of night
All to myself.

                                        Paul Hellweg

Chapter 2

The Use of Pitch

Richard Jamison

Because so many domestic tools, weapons, and other items are constructed with the use of pitch, a knowledge of how to use this essential substance is vital to every outdoorsman.

Collecting Material

To harvest pitch, search for a scarred or damaged pine tree where the sap has oozed out to form balls. Porcupines often eat the bark of pine trees, leaving large bare spots where the pitch can be collected in large quantities very easily. Check the ground also— occasionally balls of pitch will fall from the trees and become coated with dirt and twigs. Clear pitch is a sign of purity, but a little dirt or bark won't harm its usefulness.

The hardened lumps of sap take less effort to collect, although soft pitch can be scraped off with a "spatula stick" and hardened by heating, then cooling it.

The hardness of pitch will depend on the temperature to which it is heated; boiled pitch will become extremely brittle and hard when it cools. Very hard pitch looses its elasticity and is difficult to use in many situations. Various uses of the material require varying degrees of hardness.

Charcoal added to the pitch helps to bind it when it is being used as a glue and also acts as a binder, adding grit which prevents slipping between two smooth surfaces. Use only black charred wood, and grind it very fine between two stones. Add it in very small amounts to the heated pitch in proportions of about one part charcoal to eight parts pitch.

Search for a scarred or damaged tree where the sap has oozed out.

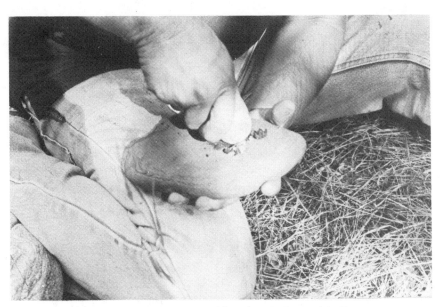

Grind black, charred wood to add to the pitch as a binding agent.

Technique

The easiest method of storing pitch is to make "pitch sticks" or "pitch twigs," the only difference being the size of the stick. Small pitch twigs are used primarily as a fire-starting aid and are lightly covered with pitch.

To make a pitch twig, first collect a number of small (3- or 4-inch) pieces of dry wood and set them aside.

Next, place one flat rock in position at the edge of the fire and lean another against it on a slight slope. Coals can then be added or scraped away beneath the sloping rock, depending on the intensity of heat desired.

Once the rock is hot enough to melt the pitch it will begin to run. Quickly roll one of the twigs in the pitch, gathering an even amount on one end.

Dip the twig in water to harden the pitch and repeat the process two or three times with each stick.

Now reverse the twig and build up an equal amount of pitch on the opposite end.

Finally, roll the pitched twigs in dirt to prevent them from sticking together while stored.

Prop a flat rock against a stone near the fire to allow the pitch to melt and run down, where it can be collected on the pitch stick.

Pitch can also be melted in an old can, but be careful not to get the temperature too high. Remember, too, that pitch is highly flammable, so never set the can in the fire, but rather in the coals.

Pitch sticks are made in the same manner as pitch twigs, except that sticks about five inches in length are used and only pitched on one end.

Once the pitch is melted, stir in charcoal and mix it thoroughly.

Repeat the rolling and cooling process until the diameter of pitch is about the size of a penny.

Don't roll the pitch stick in the dirt—you will be using it as glue for arrows and other items and you'll want to keep it as smooth and free of impurities as possible.

Once the pitch stick is finished it will be handy for many tasks, such as attaching the point to an arrow, fletching an arrow, securing a knife blade to a handle, binding the sinew on the tops of a bow, and innumerable other uses. Pitch prepared this way may be used as glue for almost any purpose that commercial glue might be used.

When using the pitch stick as glue, be sure to heat the "objects" where you want to apply the pitch; don't heat the pitch sticks. For instance, when attaching an arrow point to the shaft, pass the notched end of the arrow over the coals for a few seconds, then

A finished pitch stick will be handy for use as glue for attaching arrow points and numerous other tasks.

roll it against the pitch stick until the pitch softens enough to adhere to the arrow shaft. A small piece of soft pitch is then placed in the notch itself, and held over the coals just long enough for it to soften before pressing the point into place. The notch and arrow are then wrapped with sinew while the pitch is still soft.

Waterproofing

Tightly woven baskets can be made waterproof by pitching them inside and out. The Indian method consisted of rolling hot stones and balls of pitch inside the basket.

Leaks in a canteen can also be plugged with pitch.

Bandaids

Emergency antiseptic bandaids can be made by applying soft pitch to the cut or scraped area. A little white ash from the fire should be used to seal the pitch and prevent it from sticking or collecting debris.

Fire Starting

The friendly crackle and pop of a campfire comes from the many small explosions within the wood as the pitch ignites. This gives us a hint of its usefulness in fire-starting.

Because pitch burns with a greater intensity than wood, it is especially useful as an aid to fire making, particularly in damp or wet weather since water cannot penetrate the pitch. When you start a fire with a match, the greatest intensity comes from the initial flame; pitch intensifies the initial flame for several minutes. You cannot "start" a fire with pitch, but you can intensify the flame.

Through experimenting we have found that one piece of pitch about the size of a quarter or slightly larger will ignite in about 30 seconds and burn intensly for 4 minutes, with a lesser flame for an additional 2½ minutes, for a total of 6½ minutes burning time.

There are three ways to take advantage of pitch in fire-starting:

1. Place the raw pieces of pitch beneath the kindling.

2. Use small pitch-coated twigs about the size of a match added to a tipi fire lay.

3. Hold a larger pitch stick on one end and use it to intensify the initial flame, much as you would use a match. (Remember, you can't "strike" a pitch stick—you must already have a flame to use the pitch stick in this manner.)

Torches

Torches can be made by dipping cattail heads in melted pitch. Reeds may also be bundled together and the end dipped in the hot pitch, then wrapped on one end with bark strips and tied with cordage and dipped again.

Large pitch sticks, similar to those used as glue sticks but with a long handle, can be used as a torch. Be sure to hold the pitch stick at an angle while it is burning, because the hot pitch will melt and drip off, and could scald bare arms and hands.

Dolce Far Niente

As I idle in this meadow,
Dreaming here amid the weeds,
Guilt attempts to halt my leisure,
Spur me on to greater deeds.
You should end this intermission,
Voice of conscience ever leads.

Then another voice speaks softly,
Placid voice that ever pleads:
Take some time to scan the blue sky:
Only once, life by us speeds.
Need you join the throngs who gather
To promote their petty greeds?

Tranquil voice to give me pleasure,
Voice of all ambitious creeds,
Both have wisdom I can treasure,
Spawned from very different seeds.
(Time is never really wasted,
Only spent on different needs.)

Manning Martin
Red Lodge, Montana

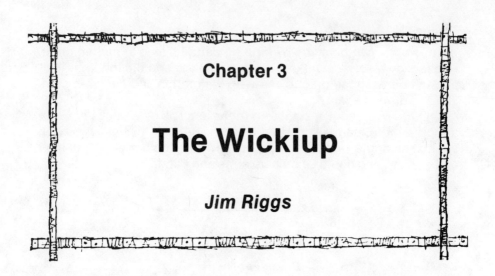

Chapter 3

The Wickiup

Jim Riggs

During a winter backpacking excursion in the Great Basin high desert of southeastern Oregon several years ago, my friend Caryn Talbot and I decided to construct a brush and pole wickiup. This was my first experience with what was to become my favorite wilderness shelter.

Wickiup? The term can bring all sorts of strange things to mind, including some rather demented puns (What are those poles for? They're to hold my wickiup!). The name may be a modification of wickiyapi, an Algonquian word from the Great Lakes region meaning lodge or dwelling, but it has evolved into a general term for many of the variously similar dwellings of aboriginal peoples throughout the western plateaus, basins and deserts.

The Nature of Shelter

All wickiups seem to have two features in common: an initial frame or skeleton of poles over which some sort of covering is affixed. Beyond that, the materials, sizes and styles vary greatly according to environmental and cultural factors. Ojibwa wickiups were pole domes covered with freshly stripped sheets of birch or other barks; Apache wickiups were often thatched with grass. Perhaps some discussion of primitive shelters, wickiups, and what we learned from our initial experience may be of value to other potential wickiup builders.

Shelter is one of man's basic needs for survival. Knowing how to construct a simple but adequate shelter, as with any bit of survival information, may someday contribute to saving your life. I believe

Spontaneous Shelters in the Great Basin

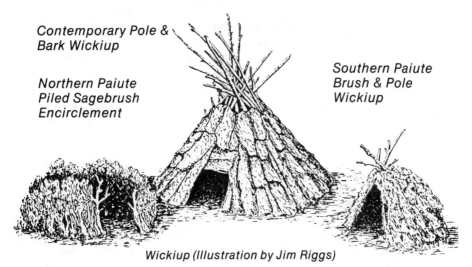

*Contemporary Pole &
Bark Wickiup*

*Northern Paiute
Piled Sagebrush
Encirclement*

*Southern Paiute
Brush & Pole
Wickiup*

Wickiup (Illustration by Jim Riggs)

the value of this knowledge is increased if one can learn to utilize available natural materials instead of relying on commercially manufactured products. By studying the ways aboriginal peoples met and satisfied their shelter needs (because their entire lives were lived in a direct relationship with their environment), we can draw from their time-tested experience.

Primitive peoples combined their human needs and ingenuity with the natural resources around them to develop shelters most suited to their lifestyles within their natural environments. Thus, the bison hide tipi (in many ways a wickiup carried to ultimate refinement) developed by nomadic horsemen of the Plains was warm, secure and adequately large, yet was dismantled and packed away in minutes should the camp suddenly need to move. The split cedar plank longhouse of the sedentary whalers and fishermen of the Northwest Coast was often structurally massive, necessarily storm-proof, and unmovable. While both of these shelter types were well adapted to their environments and uses, the manufacture of each was quite a process—the raw materials had to be obtained, then skillfully and patiently processed before they could be assembled into shelters.

By contrast, the Great Basin gatherers had neither the time nor materials to make such elaborate shelters. Since they traveled afoot, they could not carry long poles and large tipi covers even if they had them, and permanent structures were impractical because during the greater part of the year "home" was a temporary camp as they moved from one resource area to the next, taking advantage of the seasonally ripening and changing food sources.

Unlike hide tipis and plank longhouses, the simplest wickiups required no special or preworked materials; indeed, everything needed could be found growing or lying about suitable campsites. Conveniently, these places of abundant building materials were also the best camping areas because they were usually near water and, therefore, a variety of game and edible plants. Frequently the same plants provided food and construction materials.

The Brush and Pole Wickiup

Construction of the brush and pole wickiup is so easy that even a cutting implement is unnecessary! A temporary wickiup might be built for immediate protection from the elements, or it might serve as home for a week or two while a Basin family exploited a localized food supply such as a rich seed-producing plot or a productive root ground. Because many of the Basin peoples' everyday life factors were akin to what we might experience nowadays on camping, backpacking or other recreational trips, extended survival courses and treks, or the always possible unexpected survival situations, our knowledge of their simple shelters seems especially useful.

The site we chose for our first wickiup, a sage flat along a churgling, ice-filled stream a few miles up a narrow canyon in the Pueblo Mountains, abounded with dead and living cottonwood trees. Branches, limbs and poles littered the ground everywhere. The light snow cover revealed tracks and trails of deermice, wood-rats, cottontail and pygmy rabbits, coyotes and one bobcat, criss-crossing among the sages as if they were all maneuvering within a maze. Here and there we would spot where a startled bunny made an abrupt turn. One set of tracks caused me to burst out laughing; it showed how an over-eager coyote had "spun out" in his haste to catch a furry rabbit dinner! Anyway, with frequent, wind-blown snow storms and below-zero temperatures, this was a likely place to have genuinely needed to construct a survival shelter. But we mostly wanted the practice and experience of building our own wickiup.

In a flat spot adjacent to a couple of cottonwoods and big sages, we selected three long, fairly straight twelve-to-fourteen foot cottonwood poles and leaned them together to form a tripod. The two front poles were naturally forked, and we wedged them all together so the tripod stood secure without lashing. Long strips of sagebrush bark peeled from the biggest plants would have served as lashing if needed.

Caryn with cottonwood pole tripod. Tripod should be as sturdy as possible because it is the basis of the shelter.

We next dragged in many more poles and leaned them against the original tripod. Wherever possible, we jammed and wedged them into position for greater solidarity. The large ends were butted into the ground, enclosing a circular inside-floor area about ten feet across. The inside height at the center was about five feet. Smaller sticks and branches were leaned or interwoven into the spaces between the larger poles. For the doorway at the front we left open a four-foot high, rectangular space between the larger poles.

The covering or thatching should start at the bottom of the framework and progress upward so the layering effect will shed precipitation. If rain is imminent, one would be wise to construct a steeper walled wickiup than ours, but rain is generally nonexistent during the winter months in the Great Basin. Since temperatures were below zero much of the time, we were more concerned with protection from the wind. Although we achieved the desired end, we somewhat backwardly began thatching at the top of our frame and worked down, shoving successive bunches of mostly dead rabbit-bush and sagebrush under those above.

Depending on what is locally available where one builds a wickiup in northern desert areas, coverings can be bundles of

Partially completed wickiup frame of cottonwood poles.

grasses or marsh plants, sage and rabbitbush as we used, juniper and other boughs, shreddy bark—any materials having some density and bulk. Dirt, rocks and more brush are piled around the base to further block drafts. Additional poles can be leaned against the thatching to keep it from blowing off. If available, tarps or blankets can be used for further coverings. Almost anything piled on a wickiup frame will increase its weatherproofness. We eventually laid a poncho on the windward side of our wickiup and held it in place with poles. As darkness arrived and the snow fell harder, we finished

Caryn stuffs dead rabbitbrush thatching on the wickiup frame.

our first wickiup. It had taken the two of us about four hours; most of that was spent gathering thatching materials.

Ours was a large wickiup, but a smaller one would have been more practical. Determining the optimum size for a wickiup (or any shelter) is especially important in a real survival situation where conservation of energy may be critical. It should be just large enough to house the people who will use it. Ours would have easily slept six people and, with that many helping in the construction, it could have been completed within an hour. Gathering sufficient thatching was by far the most time-consuming phase. We could have greatly reduced our workload by starting with a smaller tripod and subsequently filling more of the spaces with poles and sticks before beginning the thatching. Our inexperience and eagerness to complete our shelter ahead of the increasing snowfall contributed to the lessons we learned.

Had the snowflakes been large and fluffy, I believe our wickiup would have sufficed perfectly. Unfortunately, the snow was the extremely fine kind. At first, it filtered through our not-so-thick thatching like millions of tiny commandos bent on breaking through enemy lines! To our relief it soon began to accumulate on the outside thatching and plugged its own routes. By morning, about four inches of new snow had fallen outside, while inside we experienced only a light dusting.

The author sits in the doorway of a tipi-style wickiup thatched with dead sagebrush and rabbitbrush.

Our first wickiup had protected us admirably, although the sensation of a wayward snowflake occasionally alighting on my warm neck during the night would have been less bothersome if I had been lying on a bed of warm, dry grass and shredded sagebark.

Aboriginal Values and Comforts

Wrapped snugly in my rabbitskin blanket, I dreamed with anticipation of the next day's hunt! Comfort, as we have come to know it, was not an important factor in the lives of most aboriginal hunters and gatherers; it was welcomed and appreciated when available, but not necessary nor missed.

Variations of the Basic Wickiup

The brush and pole wickiup we built is considered a temporary or summer shelter and was not normally used as a winter house by the northern Basin peoples. In fact, it was used more frequently by the southern Paiute and dwellers of the lower deserts for protection from the sun. For added cooling, they would excavate a shallow, circular depression in the ground and build the wickiup over it. The excavated dirt was then heaped around the outside base. This practice could also increase interior roominess and, in cold weather, increase heat retention inside. But, by camping in our wickiup through extreme cold, intermittent snowfalls and chilling gusts of wind, we satisfied ourselves that a simple brush and pole shelter can function adequately under winter conditions.

In preparation for inclement weather and permanent winter camp, Basin dwellers made their wickiups somewhat more substantial, but their shelters were still based on simplicity of design and materials. Several variations were common. The frame consisted of several supple willow poles set into the ground in a twelve-foot circle. The tops were generally drawn together and tied at the peak, or crossed and lashed to opposing poles to form a dome. The tipi style frame of more solid pine or cottonwood poles all leaned together was also used. Two or more rows of smaller willows were tied horizontally around the frames for bracing and to provide fastening points for the coverings. Coverings were usually large tied, twined or sewn mats of cattail, tule (bulrush), cane (phragmites), or bundles of giant wild rye grass. These mats, five or six feet wide (or as tall as the plants grew) and eight or ten feet long, were laid around the frame, bottom to top, so that they overlapped considerably for better insulation and to shed water. A smoke hole was left open at the top-center of the frame. The fire was kindled inside.

Variations in frames and coverings were nearly limitless, and depended on the materials most readily available, and perhaps even on the whims of the people. One of the simplest and best coverings was a series of "pre-fabricated" panels of willow and cattail (or tules). To make each panel, three or four willows were laid parallel, a foot-and-a-half apart on the ground. Great numbers of long cattails were laid across these (perpendicular to the willows) to a depth of six inches. More willows were laid on top, corresponding to those on the bottom. Then, at each end and every foot or so along their length, the willows were cinched and bound together through the cattails. With the cattails clamped in place, the whole panel was picked up and leaned around the frame. This type of wall was less time consuming than mat-making, and probably warmer, too. At Utah Lake in the late 1820s, mountain man Jedediah Smith wrote in his journal, "We passed through a large swamp of bullrushes, when suddenly the lake presented itself to our view. On its bank were a number of buildings constructed of bullrushes, and resembling muskrat houses. These we soon discovered to be wigwams, in which the Indians remained during the stay of the ice." It is entirely possible this type of dwelling was patterned after muskrat lodges, for we humans can learn much from the animals.

Pine pole wickiup covered with slabs of dead wood and yellow pine bark.

These winter wickiups were obviously warmer and more weather-proof than the brush wickiup, but while a single aboriginal Basin family could have probably started from scratch and completed one within a day, they might take more time and skill than a modern camper or survivalist could devote. Their simplicity is more apparent than real until one contemplates the entire manufacturing process!

The wickiups I've described here were basically adapted to desert conditions, but the wickiup-style shelter can be made any-where sufficient materials allow. In the dense forests of the south-western Oregon mountains where I lived for three years (until the rain drove me east!), a survival wickiup could be quickly constructed of downed poles and long slabs of dead cedar and fir bark. If advantageous, the whole shelter could be covered with moss, ferns, leaf litter, dirt or conifer boughs. I've many friends there who for years have been building and permanently living in innumerable variations of wickiups, pit houses and earth lodges. Even the natural sheltering qualities of hollow-based trees, upturned tree roots, large logs and boulders, dirt banks and rock shelter can be further improved with the addition of poles, bark and other materials in wickiup or lean-to style.

In any survival situation, simulated or real, you must try to do the best you can with the time and materials you have at hand. Before you begin any shelter, you should ask yourself what you expect it to shelter you from, then build it accordingly. Often the simplest combination of ideas and materials will produce the best shelter. Equally as often, it seems, there is no choice. A survival wickiup requires no preparatory thought or materials other than selecting the best spot to build it. I guess it could be called a spontaneous structure—the wickiup style is time-tested, but remains open for improvement by anyone.

The best wickiups I've constructed and lived in, since my first experience, have been during my summer courses through Malheur and Wallowa Mountain field stations, and they have proved that for temporary and quickly constructed shelters, wickiups can last for several seasons and be used over and over with only minor repairs. Large enough to comfortably house a dozen people, they were constructed of dead pine and fir poles leaned almost solidly around the original tripod and covered with large slabs of dead pine bark. Armloads of pine needles and grass were used for chinking and heaped around the outside base.

At the 1978 Woodsmoke Rendezvous, I hastily built a small (one or two person) wickiup almost entirely of dead cottonwood. It was completed in two hours. The frame was of dead cottonwood and currant branches and the covering was slabs of outer bark and long strips of inner bark peeled from downed trees which were abundant along Diamond Fork Creek. The thatching was thick and I was extremely curious as to how well it would have shed rain, but the days remained sunny and beautiful and my wickiup remained untested!

The Ready-Made Abode

Wickiups are easy to build in a rich forest environment, however, and finding or creating adequate shelter in a more marginal environment is a better test of one's abilities. Because the procurement of food was their highest priority, Basin peoples learned to accept or utilize whatever shelter was easiest and most convenient. Rock shelters (caves) served as ready-made abodes, and trees such as juniper, mountain mahogany and pinion pine probably provided welcome temporary shelter when they were to be found. But in the northern Great Basin, sagebrush provided the champion shelter.

On many flats, especially along the streams, the sagebrush reaches gigantic proportions and can afford satisfactory shelter with little or no modification. A worn area beneath one huge, umbrella-like sage near our camp was a popular deer bed. I checked this natural shelter the morning after the snow began, and less snow had accumulated there than inside our wickiup! I chuckled to think that a wise aborigine would have camped right there instead of spending a whole afternoon constructing a wickiup.

The Sagebrush Wickiup

The most common temporary shelter used by the Northern Paiute and other Basin people was made of large sagebrushes piled up waist to head high in a circle ten or twelve feet across. A door space was left in the encirclement and a fire was built in the center. Sometimes a mat, skin or blanket was rigged up for a door. Although the piled sage would often lean inward, there was no real roof. This extremely practical ring of sage is much like a frameless wickiup with an extra-large smokehole! It is further described in the 1849 journals of Basin explorer John C. Fremont, by aged informants in several Paiute ethnographic studies and in my article "Sagebrush: The Ancient Survival Kit."

Brush shelters such as this one and the brush and pole wickiup we built seldom completely stopped the wind, but served to diffuse and absorb it—to "break its spirit."

Fires for Warmth and Cooking

For cooking and warmth, we built a large fire in front of our wickiup. At the time I was leary of kindling a fire inside because of our low "ceiling," but in the numerous enclosed wickiups I've built since then, I've come to prefer an inside fire. Ours would have been a much warmer and cozier abode, and the fire's heat would have evaporated the fine snow that sifted in. One must remember to keep the fire small, burn woods that do not spark (this may take some experimentation), if possible, and never leave a flaming fire untended—once reduced to coals it is reasonably safe if protected from the wind.

For most outdoor uses I prefer a small fire built on flat ground and unringed with rocks, but for increased safety and warmth, a pit fire is most functional inside a wickiup. Sparks are less likely to fly out of the pit, and upright sticks, green boughs or rocks may be placed around the edge to further deter them. A good bed of coals left in a pit fire will soon "ash over" and can remain alive for a couple of days—a nice security when, otherwise, a new fire must be started without matches!

A wickiup built for an inside fire should have as small a door-way as is convenient—one that can easily be closed with a bush, slab of bark, etc.—for increased heat retention. An amazing amount of heat and light reflects back from the interior walls of a wickiup, even a sparsely covered one. Usually the openings where the poles cross at the top are sufficient to draw the smoke upward.

If you build your fire in front of your wickiup as we did, or have made a "half wickiup" (large, open front), a circular brush enclosure behind the fire makes for a warmer camp. Taking advantage of a couple of standing cottonwoods and live sages already present, we gathered more sage and piled up a large windbreak around our fire. The front of the wickiup served as part of the enclosure. These are windbreaks and heat reflectors while they last, but become fuel for the fire as needed. I have seen old photos showing brush wind-breaks piled all the way around tipis and grass houses, as well as wickiups.

If you should wonder about the amount of work involved in wrestling with all the sagebrush needed for thatching, windbreaks and fuel, keep in mind the old proverb, "Each sagebrush warms you twice—once when you collect it, and once when you burn it!" Had they ever been held, I believe that sagebrush wrestling should have been a major event in the Paiute Olympics.

In my experiences since building my first wickiup, I've found that the best arrangement for a group of people working, cooking and sleeping closely together in one camp for several days (as on a primitive living expedition) is the semicircular, open-fronted "half-wickiup" used in conjunction with the trench fire. The wickiup is constructed as usual, except a wide gap—perhaps a third to a half of what would be the circumference—is left open at the front. If possible, the wickiup should face away from the prevailing winds. A few feet in front of the opening a shallow (6 to 8 inch), narrow (18 to 24 inch) trench is gouged out with bones, sharp rocks or dig-ging sticks (save the excavated dirt in a pile to refill the trench when you leave). The trench length is most efficiently dug as long as the

Participants of a primitive expedition utilize the trench fire built in front of the open-front wickiup.

mouth of the wickiup is wide, leaving enough space at each end for people to move freely around the fire and into the wickiup.

The trench-style fire (and I've often made them 14 to 18 inches long) has several advantages over a "normal" campfire: Unwieldy, large-diameter poles and logs can be laid in it full-length (no need to expend energy trying to break them up) for long-burning night fires, and heat and light are reflected into the entire wickiup. More people can sleep more warmly close to the fire. Those in the wickiup are usually comfortable sleeping side by side, feet toward the fire, while those outside sleep broadside to it. I suggest that everyone make a nightly stack of firewood within easy reach—when anyone awakens chilled, he can simply stoke his section of the fire (or the whole thing if he's more compassionate and energetic!). Additional heat and light can be directed into the wickiup by constructing a reflector of piled logs, bark or brush or rocks behind the trench fire (leave enough room between reflector and fire for sleeping and moving about). Any wickiup can be made even cozier by covering the floor with a thick layer of dry grass, pine needles, bark chips and other duff for added insulation, but maintain a constant lookout for flying sparks that may land in these highly-combustible materials.

For preparing those eloquent survival meals, different sections of the trench fire can be used simultaneously for different purposes—open flames for boiling soups, stews and teas, bright coals for broiling fish and game and dying embers for baking ashcakes. I often dig a reusable rock-lined pit oven at one end of the trench and construct an above-ground rock slab oven for baking loaves of bread at the other end. But I digress—the wonders of a trench fire deserve their own article, and we're discussing wickiups here!

The Essence of Survival

The essence of survival is making do the best you can with whatever you have on hand or can get at any moment, or as put by Larry Dean Olsen in his book *Outdoor Survival Skills,* "A survivalist accepts it (his condition) as it is, and improves it from that standpoint." If you never actually need to make a survival shelter of any kind, there is a certain intrinsic value in constructing and camping in one solely for the experience . . . for the fun of it!

A shelter, especially one made from natural materials by your own hands, turns "the spot where you made camp" into a home. At the end of the day, as you return from your foraging maybe with a can full of berries, roots, a fish—maybe nothing more than your unsatiated, shriveled stomach—it is at least a warm feeling to round the bend and see your wickiup waiting. "I wonder if anybody else found anything to eat . . . maybe they brought back ALOT OF FOOD!" You are home.

Certainly a plus for the wickiup as a survival shelter is that it can best be made from dead and downed materials, colonial marsh plants or plants so abundant as sage and rabbitbush that the harvesting of a wickiup's worth is not detrimental to the plant or animal communities.

When we are thoroughly conditioned nowadays to rely on artificial or manufactured products for our sustenance, some recognition of our abilities to create useful things with nothing but our hands, minds and some raw materials seems especially valuable. Knowledge of primitive skills, combined with some common sense, may sometime be a key to survival in a modern world. For some of us, it already is.

———————————————

Two city slickers went hunting for the first time. As they left camp early in the morning, they talked about what to do if they became lost. One of them said, "If you get lost, shoot three times into the air and help will come. If no one comes in a short time, shoot three more times." Sure enough, one of the slickers got lost. When they found him two days later, tired, hungry and just a short way from camp, they asked why he didn't signal for help. "I did," he said, "I shot in the air three times. When help didn't come I shot three more times. Then I ran out of arrows."

Dallan Hendry

Chapter 4

I Wonder Where the Water Is?

Richard Jamison

Much has been written of downed pilots and lost patrols in the deserts of Africa. These accounts of suffering and death from lack of water are spine chilling and should serve to make us more aware of the importance of water, particularly in a survival situation.

When many people think of the desert and finding water they picture Gary Cooper, John Wayne or Cornell Wilde crawling across endless sand dunes, having discarded their water container after the last drop of water slowly dripped down their parched throats. I don't mean to imply that finding water in the desert is always easy, but Hollywood has given us a distorted impression of reality.

Recognizing Our Water Needs

Unless placed in an emergency situation, we seldom realize the importance of water. For instance, the first concern of most of my students is food. Food is something we can savor, chew, enjoy, and it stays with us for awhile. We also have to work to pay for the food we eat. Water, on the other hand, comes to us free, except for the monthly utility bill we are charged for transporting it to us. In restaurants we are served a glass of water, even a refill, with no charge, but seldom does anyone get a free meal.

Of course, there are different conditions, depending on the various terrains and situations in the world. My remarks will be limited to the desert areas of southwestern United States.

The desert area of southern Utah was once populated by a large number of people. This is substantiated by the number of sites and dwellings found there today. These people raised beans, corn and squash, all requiring water. They knew the importance of water and built check dams and irrigation systems for their crops. Today this entire civilization is gone. Many claim it was due to drought conditions.

Now, when people come to this part of the country for recreation, they find a scenic, semi-arid desert with very little water—at least very little that is visible to the eye. Many vacationers never leave their vehicles because of the lack of water in the area. This is a shame, because it is beautiful country to explore and hike if you are familiar with the availability of water and how to find it.

Water Indicators

If you keep your eyes open for water indicators you can find enough to satisfy your thirst and need, although there are places in the desert where water is scarce and far between. That is why you must drink all you can hold when you do locate a good source. Water will do your body no good if it is in your canteen. Of course, if you have a canteen, fill it at each water hole, but tank up before venturing on.

Large holding tanks can be found in the white sandstone canyons.

The Southwest is full of red and white sandstone. The red sandstone is very porous and does not lend itself to holding water. Don't look for water there. The white sandstone, on the other hand, holds water quite well. I have seen holding tanks 8 feet deep and 10 to 12 feet across. During the winter and early spring months, when the snow melts and the rains are abundant, water will collect in these holding tanks and stay all summer. Of course, the summer sun will evaporate some of the smaller ones.

Small potholes fill with rain water and offer another good source of water.

To locate these water pockets, you must carefully study the terrain. Cliffs with steep sides will allow water to run off at a more rapid pace and it will not collect, but water running through narrow canyons will cut out channels and pockets allowing it to accumulate. If water is not to be found on the canyon floors, look higher.

I like to get on a high vantage point and survey the indicators, such as differing shades of green, more vegetation than normal, cottonwood trees, willows, cattails, reed grass or tamarix, and canyons that might hold good possibilities. Cactus does hold moisture, but in most plants it is not easily available. It must be sucked out or the cactus cut up and used to generate moisture in a solar still.

Dry stream beds should not be overlooked. Occasionally you will find moist areas in the streambed, especially in the bends and

The view from a high vantage point will reveal bands of green which indicate water sources.

where side canyons flow into the stream. Often water will run only a short distance and disappear into the ground. It is best to dig at sharp bends in the stream because this is where the water slows down and is most likely to be trapped.

Water can also be collected from plants in early morning as the dew collects. A shirt or handkerchief will absorb the moisture, which can then be wrung out or sucked directly from the cloth.

A solar still can be used to obtain water under ideal conditions, but unless you are well equipped you probably won't have the materials necessary to build one.

Depressions in a stream bed indicate a good spot to dig for water.

Build a Seep Hole

A natural holding tank can be made with grass, stones and a piece of reed grass that will work in most instances. Dig a hole about 3 feet deep at the base of a large cottonwood tree, preferably in the bend of a dry stream bed or in moist sand. Dig the hole as close to the roots of the tree as possible. Line the hole with stones and fill it with grass. Place one end of the reed into the bottom of the hole, being careful not to imbed it in dirt, then cover the pit carefully with soil, leaving the other end of the reed protruding through the top. The tree will absorb moisture from the soil during the day and release it at night; this will be the time to check for water. Any water which may have seeped into the hole can be sucked up through the reed straw. The success of this method will depend on the area and amount of water released by the tree. It takes very little effort to construct and is worth a try if you are in need of water.

Water Is Your First Priority

Because water is your most valuable asset, you should base your camp nearby and forage for food from there. Never move long distances from your water supply unless you have located another source first. You can live for many days on water alone, but only a few days without it.

In a survival condition, don't eat any food if no water is available. Food requires moisture for proper digestion and if there is no water the body will suffer from dehydration. Remember, too, the body loses large amounts of water through perspiration. Sometimes we are not aware of these water loses because the moisture evaporates or is blown away or dried by summer breezes.

On one of our trips we had a particular student who complained alot. His biggest complaint was that he was forced (not physically, but of necessity) to drink water inhabited by pollywogs. Finally one evening his thirst got the best of him and he asked another student who was making a trip to the water hole to bring back a container of water. The fellow student smirked as he handed him his container and watched him gulp it down without a breath of air. Later he admitted that he had deliberately scooped up several pollywogs with the water. The complaining stopped and the students all collected their own "pollywog water" from that point.

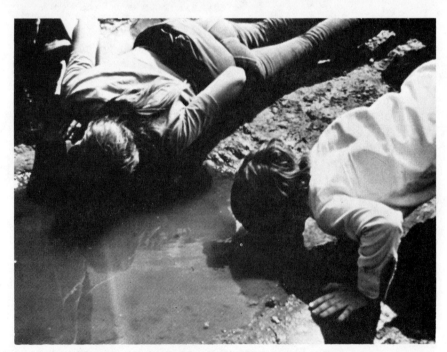

Don't be afraid to drink water that is muddy or clouded. The danger of dehydration is greater than the danger of poisoning.

Moral: If you are in a situation where water is scarce, don't be afraid of contamination. The results of dehydration are far more serious than illness caused by impure water. Most water, even though muddy or inhabited by small "creatures," is pure enough to drink. Of course, if you have proper facilities to boil your water before drinking, do so. If not, oak leaves will act as a natural purifier and charcoal from your fire will sweeten bad-tasting water.

Take Necessary Precautions

Caution must be taken by wearing sufficient clothing, such as hat, long-sleeved cotton shirt and long pants. Sure, it's cooler to wear shorts and no shirt in the summer to "beat the heat," but under survival conditions you are actually allowing the valuable water within your body to evaporate. Even if you are not "in" a survival situation, carelessness may cause one. Remember, too, lack of water will impair your judgment and ability to function properly. You will need all your faculties if you intend to make it out alive. Some of the symptoms of dehydration include fatigue, headache, poor circulation, blurred eyesight, poor judgment and lack of coordination. The treatment is: drink plenty of water and get out of the direct sun.

Interesting studies have been made of the methods of obtaining water by various tribes in Africa and other areas where water is scarce. Some tribes chew roots to obtain moisture, others drink the blood of animals, occasionally a small well will support an entire tribe. At any rate, the next time you pass a drinking fountain, take a long "free" drink and appreciate the ease of its availability.

We had a scout on a survival outing who was trying to use his watch as a compass to find the direction. He really had a time of it—seems he had a digital watch.

Dallan Hendry

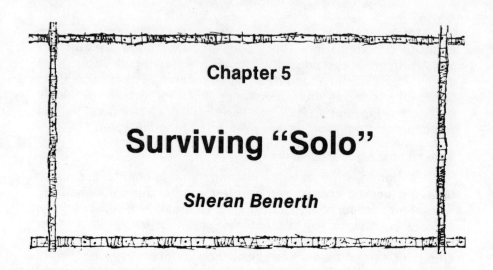

Chapter 5

Surviving "Solo"

Sheran Benerth

Editor's note: With all the thousands of survival students that have been on the trail under the direction of Larry D. Olsen, this is the only account known to us of an injurious encounter between any student and a warm-blooded wild animal. Our thanks goes to Sheran for sharing this rare experience with our readers.

Three weeks of intensive instruction on construction of traps, weapons, preparation of wild foods, climbing, rapelling, and cross-country treks were being culminated with a final week of special activities. Part of the graduation from the Youth Leadership 480 class at Brigham Young University was a 3 night 4 day solo experience.

My husband and I were students of Larry Olsen during the summer of 1968 in the southern Utah desert country. For the solo experience the class members were placed at about one-fourth-mile intervals up several different canyons. Our days of doing without were over, and for all general purposes the rest of the course should have been a cinch.

I had been placed in an area of small overhanging sandstone ledges. Water and firewood presented no problem and I had once again been issued a sleeping bag, rations and reading materials. Basically the time was to be one of reflection over past events, self-evaluation and a bit of introspection.

My first task involved clearing all the little nests out of a suitable cave-like overhang and to prepare it for my living quarters. There was enough head clearance to sit upright without receiving a concussion, but standing was out of the question. The area was about

6 feet by 12 feet, and an upshoot at one end provided a natural chimney for a convenient fire.

The remainder of the afternoon was spent surveying what was to be my home for the next four days. I was situated in a canyon with a beautiful creek flowing through the center. Steep red sandstone walls enclosed me as the sun sank behind them. A stand of cottonwood would provide a canopy of shade from the heat of the mid-day sun in the days to come. A few sage brush bushes dotted the area and there were a few sprigs of "Mormon Tea" scattered in the rock.

Evening came quickly and I built a small fire for both meal preparation and companionship. Reflection over the past course experiences filled my evening. As darkness surrounded me, the sleeping bag lying to the back of the ledge became more enticing. Sleep was slow coming as my imagination played with each sound in the void beyond. What seemed commonplace and familiar during the day almost became alien at night.

The next day my energy level increased as the sun rose higher. I quickly fixed a small breakfast and set out for further exploration. A pencil-thin slithering line through the sand showed the trail of a snake's night-time hunt along the creek. The splish-splash sounds which stirred the goose bumps on my spine the previous night were quickly explained by fresh deer tracks leading across the creek.

The remainder of my day was filled with the menial tasks of daily living and a great deal of introspection. The evening breeze was a welcome change from the sun's heat. The flames of the evening fire danced, their rhythmical moves casting shadows which over-emphasized the black void beyond the confines of the walls. Clouds screened out the moon, eliminating the mysterious outer shadows of the previous evening.

Sleep came easier my second night out. Towards morning a storm broke loose with all possible fury. Rain literally poured from the clouds, creating instant waterfalls which cascaded down through previously non-descript seams in the canyon walls. It was nature in one of her more unfriendly, yet beautiful moments. Thunder echoed through the canyons, lightning streaked across the sky, and the rain turned to hail. Almost as suddenly as the storm had begun, it was over. The solace I had found in my warm sleeping bag was no longer necessary. The air was cool and fresh. As blue sky began to appear, I meandered out to inspect the hail slowly melting on the warm sand.

As I raised from a crouched position, a movement caught my attention. There on a ledge just above me was the wettest, scrawniest-looking bobcat I have ever seen. We were about six feet from each other and were both taken by surprise. The cat bolted towards me, knocking me against the rocks. He hit me on the shoulders with his forepaws and down the front of my thighs with his back paws. Then, in a single bound he was over my shoulder and gone. Apparently thinking he was cornered, he didn't hang around to gnaw on me for breakfast.

My wounds consisted of deep scratches on both shoulders and thighs, and a loss of about ten years growth. Somewhere in the back of my mind the thought of tetanus kept creeping in. It had been years since my last shot. In fact, I didn't remember my last shot.

Our instructors assured us before our solo that they would check on us from time to time. This was comforting, but I had no idea as to whether I had already been checked that day by field glasses. My mind started to defeat me. The fear of tetanus, the loneliness, and apparently mild shock started to take their toll. All I could think of was finding help. I knew Al, my husband, was somewhere downstream.

Not much is clear after that point, until I remember Al taking me by the arm and leading me into his camp. He placed me in his sleeping bag and fixed some broth. He had heard me calling his name and found me following the creek downstream. He was sure I would never break the solo assignment unless something was wrong. My arms and legs were caked with blood, which must have made quite a gruesome impression. As I began to become a bit more coherent, I tried to relate my tale.

I was starting to stiffen up and ache, but Al agreed I needed a tetanus shot. The only way out was to walk. We started back upstream and about an hour later hit the jeep trail we had been brought out on. The sun seemed relentless and beat on us unmercifully. Then in the distance we spotted a car coming toward us. Larry and another instructor were coming out to check on the students. The drive back to the ranch, where we had left our car, seemed terribly long, and the initial feeling of panic kept trying to return. We drove to the nearest doctor, who was in Panguitch, Utah—90 miles away.

After a good examination, some first aid and a tetanus shot, we were on our way back. During the course of the exam, the doctor told me that if there were any bites I might be facing rabies injections. All he found were scratches.

We reached the main camp late that afternoon. Larry and the rest of the instructors met us and discussed the earlier events of the day. There was one more night left to finish out my solo. I must admit, though, I really didn't relish the thought of going back out. Except for the scratches I really felt fine, so after a little joking and coaxing I agreed to go out and finish my solo. We drove out to the canyon and I settled in for the night. Sounds again played with my imagination, but the full moon and the stars helped keep everything in perspective. The night was clear and cool. Crickets chirped their nightly serenade and the peacefulness eventually turned into a sleep of tranquility.

Solo was over and, despite the altercation with the bobcat, it was a worthwhile experience. Seldom do we have the opportunity to be completely alone in our modern society. It is a challenge to overcome loneliness and fears when dependent on one's own resources.

Survival Swirls

For a nourishing food that tastes good too, Survival Swirls are right for you.

A good survival food is easily made with three ingredients. Flour, water and anything edible from nature—plant or animal.

Flour can come from many sources—most seeds and grains can be made into flour as well as cattail heads and roots. The roots of many plants make excellent flour when roasted and ground.

Once the ingredients are at hand, the rest is easy. . . . First make a stiff dough of flour and water and knead it a few times. Mold it into a long thin cigar-shaped piece about one to two feet long. Next wrap it around a stick that has been skinned of its bark. Seal the end by pinching it together with a little water so that the stick doesn't show through. Also seal any cracks completely with the dough.

Now bake the dough over the flames of a fire until golden brown. Pull it off the stick carefully and into the resulting cavity put the third ingredient. This can be greens, either cooked or raw (even the bitter ones are edible when prepared in this way) or meat or fish that has been cooked in advance are especially tasty.

For a special treat fill the hole with brown sugar or honey, dates or raisins.

Umm umm good!

Kim Smith

Chapter 6

Keep a Fine Grind and a Level Bevel

Cecil Hamilton

My experience as a butcher for sixteen years has inspired me to pass on some information that I feel is very important not only to survivalists, but to anyone who loves the outdoors and uses a knife.

During my years as a "knife man," it has been important for me to know what makes a knife cut well, so I have done a lot of experimenting on different sharpening methods.

Obtaining a Flat, Sharp Edge

The method I finally have settled on involves a magnifying glass. When I hone a knife a certain way and look at the edge through the glass, I can tell whether I have a good edge or not. I have found that if you put the knife on the honing stone tip-first and grind to the base of it, the result is a wire edge. When drawn back, the motion takes the wire edge off, leaving it nice and smooth. I have also discovered that by adding a slight twist of the wrist and of the stone at the tip of the knife, even the tip will sharpen like the rest of the blade.

Most people sharpen a knife in a circular motion. This doesn't produce a truly sharp edge. The magnifying glass reveals a thin, feathery edge from this method. I also found that when I used the back and forth "sawing" method, the edge was rounded instead of having a flat sharp edge.

When the tip of the knife is put on the stone, it should not be too flat. When this happens, the blade becomes scratched and will drag through whatever you are cutting. The angle at which the knife is held to the stone has long been a subject of argument among outdoorsmen, but I have found that if you maintain enough of an angle

Keeping the knife at the proper angle will result in a sharper edge.

Starting from the tip, grind to the base.

With a twist of the wrist and of the stone, even the tip will sharpen like the rest of the blade.

that you are not actually on the blade or the bevel, but rather on the edge, you will have better luck.

There is another aspect of sharpening a knife that is important—that is removing a nick or low spot caused by grinding. Start the knife on the stone at the tip, then go to the base and back several times on each side, then on the opposite side until the nick is removed. Finish the job by sharpening from tip to base and back, only on alternate sides, until you have honed it smooth.

Choosing a Sharpening Stone

You will want to choose your stones carefully; it will probably be a one-time purchase unless you misplace them. If you are using your knife to cut meat you will want both a 120 grit carborandum and also an extremely smooth stone. If you are working on wood, use only the rough stone. The grit is for grinding the edge; the smooth stone serves to remove the wire edge. This can also be done on a leather belt or razor strap.

Knife Safety

When honing a knife, don't get in a hurry. It's easy to slip the blade under the stone and cut yourself.

Never hand a knife to someone by holding the blade. Hold the bottom of the handle with the back of the blade between your thumb and forefinger. Then, when it is taken, even if the blade touches you, you won't be cut.

Always keep a pocket knife closed when not in use. Keep a sheath knife in the sheath when not in use.

I know from my own dealings with survival, backpacking and outdoor crafts, that a good knife is the most utilitarian tool a person can have. When you have a sharp knife, it will function better and make your crafts more artistic.

I want to retain the peace I found away from it all. And I want to go back every so often to find that peace again. Now that I know it exists, I want to be able to find it in other places, perhaps even in crowded places.

Survival Student

Chapter 7

Surviving a Blizzard With Only a Blanket

Larry J. Wells

The glint of a bright February sun reflecting from the crystal snow made it difficult to photograph the pair of immature Golden Eagles. Smoothly they soared above the large black basalt cliff, rising, dropping, their eyes searching the juniper and sagebrush of Meadow Creek Canyon.

Although it is not a heavy snow year in southeastern Idaho, two feet of the glistening frozen crystals cover the drainage of Willow Creek, site of the Ririe Dam. Steve Anderson, Burnell Walker and myself are on our way to Deer Creek, another tributary of Willow Creek, to photograph deer and elk in their winter range before the Ririe Dam is completed and their winter range is buried by water. As a sidelight we are going to try some cold weather survival techniques.

These beautiful young Golden Eagles are a welcome bonus. Slowly they drop, rise, turn and drift over the rocky sagebrush ridge. Their search for food, so far, is in vain.

Our yellow and white International Scout pitches and tosses us around as it churns through the snow, climbing the dugway out of Meadow Creek to the dry farms above. The end of the road is a large hard-packed snow drift. After turning the Scout around so we are heading downhill (just in case of starting problems later), we quickly put on our packs, anxious to find the game animals and set up camp.

The snow we thought would be scoured off the dry farms by the wind is not. Snow clutches at our boots adding torture to the quickly tiring legs. Our lungs suck the crisp air, burning, coughing. As far as we can see are rolling hills, covered with what appears to be shimmering frosted glass. Patches of naked Quaking Aspen trees are the only break in the glistening world of white. A drop of sweat hits my

52

sun glasses—time to shed more clothes; for the second time I start to undress.

Faintly we hear a mild buzz—snow machines. We grumble . . . "No peace on earth left." Then, as they draw near, I recognize them. We realize it is manna from heaven in disguise of vibrating, offensive noise-makers.

Bouncing across the crusted snow at 40 mph sure beats stumbling through at ½ mph with charlie horses playing leap frog up and down your legs. In just minutes we are to the rim of Deer Creek, saying good-bye and thank you to Bob and Alice Harris.

No sooner do we step to the rim, but fifteen head of mule deer break out below us, jumping, running, trotting through the junipers, breaking limbs and kicking rocks down the hill.

Now to find a campsite. I have two wool blankets, Steve and Burnell have light sleeping bags. If we are to be comfortable we will have to be careful in our location and preparation.

The snow on our side of the canyon wall, a south exposure, is patchy, with drifts here and there among the basalt boulders and juniper trees. Across Deer Creek are dry farm fields blanketed with snow. The canyon is dressed with sagebrush and juniper, with cottonwood trees lining the creek.

A small cove looks like it would give wind protection on three sides, and it is in the thermal belt or middle third of the slope. There are dead standing juniper for dry firewood, a large snowbank behind a boulder for water, and dry ground in front of another good-sized lava rock for my coal bed site. Big clumps of bunch grass (wild rye) are just up the hill for ground bedding material and we should get the early morning sun since nothing is in the east to shade us. This looks like home.

After shedding clothes, to air out and keep from being cold later, I start digging a trench for my coal bed. When there are low temperatures a coal bed is the key to staying warm all night without feeding a fire. I dig it as long as my body, a couple of feet wide, and a foot deep (see illustration). Thank heavens the soil is soft—I am able to easily scoop it out with a flat rock. The smell of new-turned earth is pleasant.

Since temperatures have ranged between -5° and -15° the last few nights, I make a reflector fire trench as long as my body as a back up system.

Steve and Burnell have decided to share a common ground cloth so they can use their other one for a cover should it snow (the clouds are already building up). They level an area large enough for two by building a crib with wood and rocks and filling it with dirt.

I start the fire in my coal bed trench, which must burn long enough to gain a thickness of 3-4 inches of glowing-hot coals, covering the bottom of the trench. I would have covered the trench bottom with flat rocks before building the fire to help hold the heat, but none were available. Fragrant cedar smoke rises from the snapping juniper and drifts over the area.

With their sleeping platform made, Steve and Burnell help me spread the hot embers evenly over the bottom of the trench (any high piles of coals might result in a "hot spot" during the night like in the movie "Jeremiah Johnson"). We then place a six-inch cover of dried dirt over the embers. After laying down a plastic ground cloth to keep moisture out, we add the finishing touch—a layer of bunch grass.

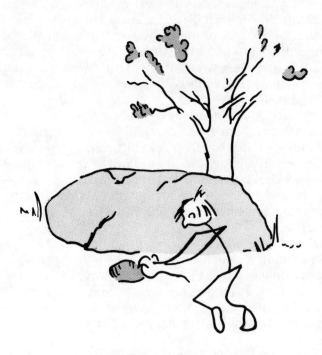

1. *Scoop out trench the length of body, two feet wide, and one foot deep.*

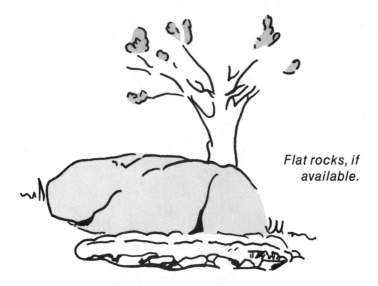

Flat rocks, if available.

2. *Dry, basalt rocks have less chance of exploding.*

3. *Fire full length of trench until three to four inches of coals cover the bottom of the trench.*

4. *Spread the coals evenly over the bottom of trench.*

5. *Cover with six inches of the driest dirt available.*

6. *Cover with ground cloth to keep steam off your bed or let it steam out for two to three hours.*

   Note: Never make a coal bed unless necessary as it does sterilize the ground for a period of time.

Triangle Blanket Wrap

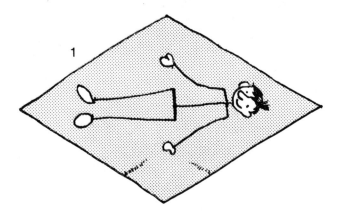

2

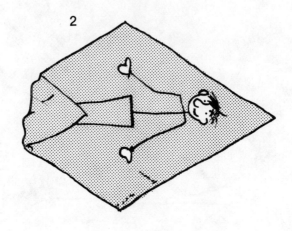

3

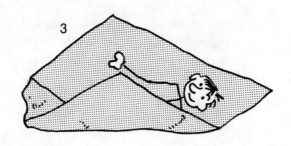

4

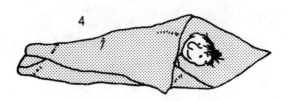

After a supper of rice, T.V.P., ashcakes, and raisin turnovers (ashcakes over raisins and brown sugar) we settle down for the night. Using the Indian or triangular blanket wrap (see illustration), I wrap up in my blankets on top of the coal bed.

The clouds have blown over and millions of stars twinkle and sparkle in the black sky, sending their ancient light of eons ago to bounce off the mass of frozen snowflakes. A glowing, cold white full moon rises to give an eerie sheen to the snowcrusted ridges and fields, deep shadows form in the gullies. The temperature drops to -5° and ice starts to form on my beard. Coyotes give a final chorus, punctuated several times by owls calling back and forth, and I drift to sleep.

Something wet on my face—my dreams say it's rain—SNOW! Automatically I start to sit up. OW! My beard is frozen to the blanket. The moisture from my breath has joined the two in a bond of ice. As I listen to the wind screaming over the dry farms, I grope for the other half of my ground cloth to pull over my blanket. After a few handfuls of gorp to produce body heat, I pull the wool stocking hat down over my face and snuggle against the warm bed underneath me, where the hot embers are still doing their job.

My mind slowly begins to stir—first noticing the heavy weight on my body. It feels like grandma's heavy denim quilts. Then a runner comes from my feet to my brain to say they are colder than they should be. As I peek from under my wool cap, the first thing to greet me is three inches of wet snow. That explains the weight, and a quick look to see my feet poking out into the snow explains their problem. Steve and Burnell are just a lump in the snow.

After muttering, moaning and groaning, we are all out from under the snow and standing around a struggling fire made from dry wood which Steve stashed the night before. I soon find out I was far warmer with blankets on the coal bed (I didn't need the reflection fire) than they were in their sleeping bags.

When Herman Schluter and his wife Mary came in on snow machines to see if we were okay we found we had slept through the worst blizzard of the winter, with temperatures in town of -8° and winds up to 40 mph (no wind was in the cove). The schluters had talked to Bob Harris and knew we were out in the storm. They felt sure they would find us frozen to death.

It had been a good learning experience of what can be done with very little help from civilization if you take the time and proper preparation.

Now to find the game and get the pictures we were after.

Chapter 8

Surviving Winter Hazards

Larry J. Wells

Several times a season we read about the hunter who sees the big buck, blasts away, and then runs into the chase after only wounding the animal. In his excitement he leaves his "survival gear" in his vehicle. A storm catches him or he becomes lost. We read of snowmobilers who have mechanical problems or become lost in an unexpected blizzard. Most of these stories do not have happy endings.

The key to winter survival is the old scout motto: "Be Prepared."

One winter through an almost tragic experience, I found just how important preparation can be.

A neighbor asked me if I would get a red fox out of a hole for him. He shot the fox and it had crawled into its hole and died. My neighbor had been unable to get him out.

I took my two sons, Monte, age 10, and Torren, age 7. It was a beautiful, crisp January morning. After locking up the land cruiser we began our walk across the flat dry farm field to the creek bank the neighbor had described as the place where we would find the fox hole.

Being only a fourth of a mile away, we were walking the bank of the creek in a short time and soon found the hole in a side irrigation ditch bank on the side of the dry farm field.

We had only been there a short while when the overcast sky started dropping down and the wind began to blow. The wind increased, dropping the windchill below zero. Soon the wind was howling. There was no shelter available so I decided to get the boys back to the car and out of the cold.

When we were a hundred yards from the ditch, a ground blizzard closed in. Moisture added to the wind chill and our world had neither up nor down, only white. Our faces turned crimson and my beard formed a layer of ice.

Torren began to shiver as the wind cut through his jacket. I asked them if they had their face masks. They didn't. I gave mine to Torren and tied a bandana over Monte's nose and chin, which by now had turned blue.

Looking around I could only see twenty feet at the most. Small crystals of ice scoured our bodies and stung our exposed flesh. There was no protection. The field was covered with a shallow three to four inches of snow crusted around the stubble. There were no drifts, no bushes, no depressions—nothing to get out of the killer wind.

I knew the highway was in a general north direction (I hadn't bothered to take a compass bearing when I left the vehicle as I could see the quarter mile to the creek—what was the use?).

Putting the boys on the down-wind side of me, I began following my compass due north.

Unexpected mechanical problems can strand motorists in severe winter storms. The secret to survival is . . . be prepared!

By the time we reached the highway about a quarter mile down from our vehicle, Torren was getting slow and stiff. We were frozen cold. Our fingers and toes cried for warmth. The wind side of our bodies were numb.

Our lives had been saved by a 98¢ compass (now $1.50). We could have died within one-fourth mile of a major highway, within two miles of our home. Without face coverings we would have had frostbite.

Carry a Winter Survival Kit

There are some very basic items you should carry with you in the winter any time you leave your home or vehicle, if only to go down the hillside:

● **Matches** in a waterproof container plus some type of windproof fire starter (highway or railroad flares work well). Cold, stiff, numb fingers make it hard to use matches, especially in the wind.

● **Compass** is a necessity in the winter time. Take a bearing when you leave your vehicle. I could have saved a frozen quarter-mile walk if I had, even though it seemed ridiculous at the time. If I hadn't known a general direction, the compass would have been of no value.

● **Face mask, ski mask, or snowmobile mask,** anything to break the wind and keep your face covered. Remember, exposed flesh can freeze in one minute at -25 degrees. This temperature is reached if it's 10 degrees above zero with a 20-mile-an-hour wind, and that isn't an extreme condition at all.

● **Wind breaker**, jacket, rain coat, anything to stop the wind. Wind kills. It brings hypothermia and frostbite to your body with amazing speed.

● **High energy food** to give the body something to burn for heat. Something to help in a pinch such as nuts, candy bars, gorp, etc. Keep in mind that

Carbohydrates burn quick for quick energy but burn up fast.

Proteins take longer to start burning but last longer.

Oils or fats are slow to burn but are long lasting. A combination of all three is best. That is why pemican is so effective.

● **Ground cloth**, something light but waterproof to keep you off the snow if you have to dig in. It can also serve as an emergency wind shelter. A rain poncho works well.

● **Knife**, the most useful tool you can have in any wilderness situation.

This is a very basic list of items that can save your life. You should, of course, be dressed for the occasion with layers of warm clothing. Wool and the new polarguard, fiber II or holofill materials are the best for winter conditions. You should have warm, water-proof or water resistant foot gear and, of course, mittens and a wool cap that will cover your ears. Eighty percent of your body heat goes out through your head if it isn't covered. A hood on your jacket is good because it covers your neck, another great heat-loss area. A bandana or scarf will take care of the neck also.

Another handy item in your pocket is toilet paper or Kleenex. A dripping nose will freeze much faster than a dry one.

This information is for basics to be carried hunting or on a short hike. Winter camping and winter expeditions require much more extensive preparations and a thorough understanding of cold weather survival.

Remember—the secret in the winter is BE PREPARED!

Some people's idea of survival is to go all night without turning on their electric blanket.

Dallan Hendry

It was a great feeling to look out at the desert and the mountains and say to myself I've been there and I overcame. Yet it wasn't a feeling of having beaten or conquered, but a feeling of understanding and appreciation.

Survival Student

Sometimes it was almost too challenging to really look at the situation I was in and find the answers, but it was this trial and error environment that really helped the most. It was indeed a very strong challenge to know that whatever I gained was going to be through my own initiative.

Survival Student

Chapter 9

Nature's Yeast

Linda Jamison

Ever run out of yeast in the middle of a batch of something? Next time you do, rush out to your nearest Aspen tree and harvest some!

Well, it isn't quite "that" simple, but yeast is available in its natural state all around us, and it *can* be used for baking if you know the technique.

My own first experience with wild yeast harvesting took place while I was working as an assistant instructor during a primitive living expedition a few years ago. A lot of interesting ideas and experimenting came about as a result of living in a semi-suffering state, not the least of which is the opportunity to field test a bounty of wild foods.

When I say "field test," I don't mean that we just eat things growing thereabout— we also teach the ancient arts of making things from plant fibers in addition to wild food preparation, and on this particular trip, we learned to collect and use wild yeast.

First I should tell you that at the beginning of each expedition we give the student a ration of whole wheat flour mixed with a lump or two of raw sugar. This is intended as a suppliment to our wild diet. The flour is mixed with water and then formed into a tortilla-like cake and baked in the ashes, becoming, you guessed it, an ashcake! I tell you this so you will understand the stimulus behind the search for something more tantalizing. Don't get me wrong, ash cakes are fine for the first day or two, even three, but by the eighth day they get a little blah.

The berries of the Oregon Grape (Berberis) have a white coating, or yeast, which can be used as leavening.

As luck would have it, one of our group was a biochemist. During our regular foraging hike he pointed to the white "film" covering the berries of the Oregon Grape (Berberis aquifolium) and explained that this was atmospheric bacteria, or yeast, which is always in the air but collects more readily on some plants than others. He also cited the example of the white powdery coating found on the trunks of Aspen trees.

The mention of yeast perked my ears. I had read about pioneers using the bark of trees to make wild yeast, but never considered using it myself, mainly, I suppose, because of the availability of the commercial product. Now, with plenty of experimenting time and a lot of motivation, I set my goal on a batch of wild yeast sourdough.

Our mouths watered in anticipation as we gathered the ingredients which were to eventually delight our palates. We collected a dozen or so Oregon Grape berries, put them into a quart-sized glass jar, which was confiscated from an old abandoned cabin near our camp, and added about a cup of our whole-wheat flour. Next we stirred in an equal amount of warm water (one cup) and screwed the lid on loosely (a tight-fitting lid won't allow for escaping gas). A "guardian," who ironically was a baker by trade, was assigned to keep vigilant watch over our experiment. He even slept with the jar to keep it warm at night.

After two days of careful watching, we knew the yeast was were elated—it actually worked!

The Finished Product

The next step was to add about a cup of the starter to approximately six cups of whole-wheat flour and enough water to make it easy to handle. We also turned the job of kneading over to our baker. We had come this far and didn't want to botch the job now.

There was nothing more to do except wait for it to rise. Well, you know what they say about a watched pot—it took three hours for that dough to rise 1½ inches on warm rocks; hardly the same action you could expect from the ordinary kitchen variety of sourdough. Nevertheless, our enthusiasm was not dampened.

I instructed the students in building a stone oven by placing a large flat rock directly into the coals of our cooking fire and enclosing the sides with stones about 18 inches in length by 8 inches high and 3 to 4 inches thick. Another large flat rock was used to cover the enclosure. We put the sausage-shaped loaves on the oven floor and closed the door with a final stone. The heat was regulated by pushing and scraping the coals from the fire surrounding the oven.

Finally, after an hour of drooling and torturing ourselves by inhaling the aroma—hurrah!—the wilderness piece de resistance: two golden hot loaves of sourdough bread. They were a perfect compliment to our meal of smoked trout and steamed watercress. Needless to say, they didn't last long.

The next day we tried mixing our sourdough starter a little thinner for pancakes, but didn't really get the results we had hoped for. Nevertheless, with a little thimbleberry juice for syrup we

Our piece de resistance . . . wilderness sourdough baked in a stone oven.

managed to devour our caveman flapjacks in short order. Later, we replenished our starter by adding a cup of flour, equal water and another handful of berries for good measure. We also mashed a few thimbleberries and added them to the mixture, hoping that the sugar in the fruit would further activate the yeast plants.

Wild Starter Experimentation

Since that time, I have done some experimenting with various types of wild yeasts in the sanctity of my own kitchen. I have found some "starts" activate well, while others are a complete flop. Through trial and error I have discovered one basic factor necessary for good wild starter—heat! Too much will kill the yeast plant, while too little heat makes the starter dormant. For the best controlled atmosphere during the night, I set my oven on warm (about 120°) and open the door. With the jar sitting on the top of the oven, toward the back, it seems to stay about the right temperature during the night.

I use the same ingredient measurements for my kitchen wild starter that we used on the trail, and add a little raw sugar to increase the yeast activity. The flavor isn't quite the same as regular home-made sourdough—it's a little more sour because it takes quite a bit longer to activate. It also tends to take on the flavor of the yeast-collecting plants if they aren't removed from the jar after the yeast has activated. Some plants will spoil after a period of time and ruin your starter if not removed.

Because it's more fun to watch it "work," I like to use a piece of plastic wrap and a rubber band or screw cap to cover the jar. I indent the top of the plastic wrap about two inches to give it plenty of room for expansion. Once the yeast starts to work, the plastic will bulge out until it seems like it will burst. Then you "know" it's working. If the flour and water separate during the process, just stir the mixture gently.

Additional Sources of Wild Yeast

Although Oregon Grape works well, I have been equally impressed with other plants for wild yeast collecting. Juniper berries also collect a useable amount of wild yeast plants. In fact, I found that it worked faster than the Oregon Grape in my kitchen laboratory.

My husband experimented with Juniper berries while on the trail in southern Utah by mixing a few handfuls of flour, some berries, and a little water in a plastic bag. After a few hours in the hot sun, the bag exploded.

Aspen trees are another good source of wild yeast. You can see the yeast "coating" by wiping your hand across the trunk of the tree. A few pieces of bark added to your flour mixture will give the desired results.

Once activated, you can use wild starter in any sourdough recipe. Just give it a little more time to rise, and don't expect it to produce the same texture and high-rising results you would get when using a commercial yeast. Be sure to replenish your starter each time you use it by adding equal parts of flour and water. Remember, too, that the more often it is used, the better it will become.

Granted, it's not as easy as opening a package of Fleischmann's, but then "natural" goodness is justified by its added sense of accomplishment.

––––––––––––––

I found it amazing, especially in myself, that even though I felt that it was impossible, the motivation was still there. I now know that this old body of mine will go further and do far more than I ever thought it could. I've discovered for myself what it means to incorporate into one's own life the meaning of the old phrase "Never say die."

Survival Student

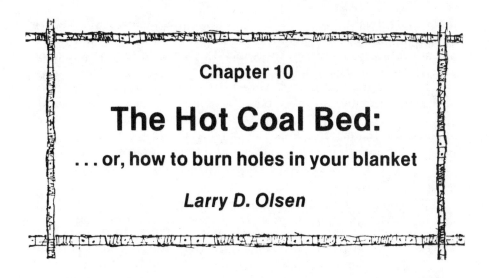

Chapter 10

The Hot Coal Bed:

...or, how to burn holes in your blanket

Larry D. Olsen

It's a wondering sight (not to mention the sounds) to watch a sleeping person suddenly rise straightupendicular, seemingly propelled by a force which leaves a trail of smoke and sparks; awake in orbit, ripping and tearing the air to shreds, and then to, at last, settle to earth with a bewildered, helpless air of embarrassment.

I suppose my slumber has been interrupted in such fashion on at least a hundred occasions. Each time the condition has been identified without question—squirming! That's it! No other sleeping action could so interrupt such a tranquil condition upon a hot coal bed. If there is anything in the wilds I'm an expert at, it's hot coal beds, and I can testify that only squirming produces such spectacular results.

I remember one night when there were thirteen of us bedded down on a community hot coal bed, toasty as a bunch of potatoes under ashes. I had taken great pains to ensure the proper depth of insulating dirt between the hot rocks and the bedding material of dry grass. Furthermore, the group received a stern sermon on the virtues of not squirming.

"Hipholes are not permitted on community hot coal beds, and moving around too much not only keeps the others awake, but also scrapes away the insulating dirt," I warned.

Sure enough, not an hour had passed before the center occupant levitated, releasing from under him that telltale smell of burning wool. (Each of us was wrapped in a single wool blanket.) He was lucky. The burn hole was only as big as a pumpkin, and his hip was only first degree. I burned up only fifty minutes of tongue lashing on the inept bunch of squirmers, telling them that civilization and soft beds had surely ruined them for the good life under the stars and I was certain that unless they all practiced better P.M.A. (positive mental attitude) and quit squirming, chances were we would all be roasted before morning.

Well, I was right. At midnight some guy near the middle yelled, "Fire!" Someone else beside me mumbled something about a steam bath and the next thing I knew there was whooping all over the place with sparks and smoke streaming in every direction. I noticed three or four red glowing patches of light streaking toward the creek. I really was disgusted.

Grabbing my blanket, I stalked off into the brush, curled up under a big juniper tree, and pleasantly cooled off for the rest of the night. I awoke once to break an icicle off my nose, and noticed that there was alot of talking going on over in the camp, and there were standing silhouettes around the campfire.

By the next morning the guys had it all figured out. It seems that the whole group (except me—I was sleeping on one end slightly apart from the rest) would squirm at the same time, being so tightly packed, and the "roll-over" game resulted in everyone reaching hip-hole depth at the same time.

It snowed the next night. We each built our own hot coal bed and only nine of the most civilized men squirmed themselves into orbit. We were on the trail for only one month, and considering that these guys were better-than-average learners, the death toll from sleeping was zero.

They were bragging about that on the last day, until I reminded them that there was only one blanket left—mine. Furthermore, they looked like a bunch of Austrailian aborigines (Austrailian aborigines are famous for their really incredible burn scars from sleeping in their campfires), and in spite of the fact that only three of them had burned off most of their hair, still they all had lost some hair. However, since they had managed to live for thirty nights under such pleasant circumstances, I finished my remarks with a hearty commendation for their efforts and said that I felt like our experience had drawn us together like brothers and that they were all welcome to go back into the wilds with me again sometime. That was five years ago. So far I haven't heard from any of them. I've concluded that they were all a bunch of cowards after all.

Chapter 11

Deadfall Trapping

Larry D. Olsen

There are those today who for humane reasons are opposed to the trapping of animals. Unfortunately, this opposition sometimes tries to identify all trapping activities as a big reign of terror upon the animal kingdom.

For a variety of justifiable reasons, animals often must be killed. Whether it is done for economic reasons or simply to survive in the wilds, trapping is still one of the most humane ways to quickly kill an animal—if it is done responsibly.

Responsible trapping implies competency, and every would-be trapper should be well acquainted with the best and most humane methods of trapping animals.

Ranking humaneness and the effectiveness of traps side by side shows us that the most humane is also the most effective. Any trap that simply "holds" is ranked lowest in effectiveness. Traps that kill quickly are ranked highest in effectiveness and should be considered first, if not exclusively, as the method of catching an animal.

Deadfalls

Deadfalls rank the highest in effectiveness. They kill instantly, and usually without damage to the pelt. They are time consuming to construct, but once in place, they may be used indefinitely. With a quantity of light-weight triggers, a trapper may travel a great distance, constructing the heavy parts from materials already existing in nature. Steel traps and snares are only superior if the area affords no natural materials for deadfalls.

Trapline Procedures

The timing necessary to operate a deadfall trapline is quite different under survival conditions as compared to conventional traplines using steel traps. Many times, students report to me that their traplines are too time consuming to be effective, because only six or seven good deadfalls can be set up in the late afternoon. Their problem is that deadfall lines should be set up according to a set-check pattern which increases the number of sets each day until a good line of about one hundred traps are in operation. Set-check traplines work this way:

Triggers

On the first day, construct as many triggers as you need for the entire line. This could range anywhere from fifty to two hundred traps, depending on your situation. Rarely can you catch enough to survive on with less than twenty traps. A hundred or more well-planned sets will keep you in plenty of meat and skins for survival. The size and strength of the triggers should be fairly standard with a catch range geared to trip on a mouse as well as a fat rockchuck. Then, whether you make a set for a small or a medium-sized animal, your triggers will all be interchangeable. At least a few triggers should be larger and stronger. They should be kept separate for the occasional opportunity to trap larger animals like fox, coyote, or even bear. These are rare, however, and more meat can be obtained by trapping the more prolific and less cautious rodent populations.

When your triggers are all made, bundle them in groups of five, and pack them for easy access on the trail.

Bait

Bait should be carefully planned and cared for. Many well-planned traplines have fallen short because of insufficient bait to finish out the line in an area where bait is scarce. For most rodents, anything salty or juicy will work as bait. A dough made from ground-up grass seeds or regular flour is best. Small chunks of hard fat, cooked meat, pine nuts, ripe cactus fruits, baked edible roots, and fresh-dried bundles of hay made from clover, dandelion, or other succulent plants will work as bait.

The trick in some cases is to keep from nibbling away at the bait yourself, before your traps are all out! When bait is unavailable, sets can be made to trip on contact using a bright object as a lure, or as a trail set through which an animal must pass and trip the set.

Setting the Traps

To place one hundred deadfalls initially will take approximately three days of fairly constant effort. On day one, start the line up one side of a canyon or valley, concentrating on the most plentiful types of animals in the area—which are usually small rodents. Place your sets at frequent intervals and in places frequented by the animals. Check signs carefully to be sure they are not old and try to see a pattern of behavior in the animals' travels. For instance, in the desert, large mice and rats are abundant. They establish runs along the base of cliffs and rocky areas, but range out into the sandy areas for food gathering. It is obvious that the rocks afford the most protection, and if food were available there, the rodents would prefer to remain near that protection. Also, in the rocks, they are less cautious and more liable to enter a deadfall set. Placing trap sets nearest their natural runways is therefore more successful than open-ground sets near where they feed at night.

Try to construct each deadfall from stones found in the immediate area. This saves a lot of hard work and also makes a less conspicuous set. Select the best possible site and make sure that the set is constructed in a permanent fashion. Any set that destroys itself upon its initial fall is not worth the effort. It must last through several successive settings. A firm base is essential and a permanent easy balance should be achieved. Rickety sets that need repeated, time-consuming balancing each time it's reset will be inefficient in the long run. By taking the time initially to shape the stone by knocking off an edge or building a firm base for it to rest on, many hours will be saved later on. Fencing around deadfalls is essential and it should be well done. Natural materials from the immediate site are best.

Proceed in a definite pattern and direction in setting out the trapline. A careful accounting should be kept on where each set is located, and some signs should be left along the main trail to indicate where and how many sets are in a given general area.

The best locator sign is simply to set one rock on top of another beside the main trail, with small pebbles placed around it—one for each trap set in the immediate vicinity.

Approximately thirty traps can be set out in this fashion on the first day in a line ranging from a mile to over five miles. It is best, however, to restrict the range to less than three miles, or about ten traps per mile. In areas where small animals are abundant, as many as thirty traps may be effective over and over again in a short one-mile stretch. This reduces the time needed to check them and saves energy as well.

On the morning of the second day, quickly check your first thirty traps. Reset the tripped sets, improve those needing improvement and return to camp with your catch. Process the catch, eat, and then travel up the opposite side of the canyon or valley, setting out another thirty or forty deadfalls.

On the third morning, early, check all the traps, process the catch, eat, and repeat the pattern of the second day, only this time set the rest of your traps in a proximate location to areas of good catches from the previous two days. This insures a greater yield in the days to come without extending the area of the trapline. From that point on, the line is maintained by checking it each morning, resetting the traps that are sprung, and processing the catch. This can all be done in about three hours if the trapline is not over three miles long. Time should be taken to pull traps that do not produce and construct new sets in a new location if necessary. A few extra replacement triggers should always be carried along with new bait. Some sets will fall on the triggers and break them.

Survival with traps is the surest way to get meat. The trapline will bring you ample food for your effort in the long run, since it is working for you while you are sleeping. That kind of economy can't be beat. The major daylight hours of gathering plant foods, hunting, drying meat and other chores of surviving are not seriously interrupted by a trapline that is checked early in the morning.

The deadfall traps shown are chosen from many forms. They are proven methods and my first choice for all areas and terrains.

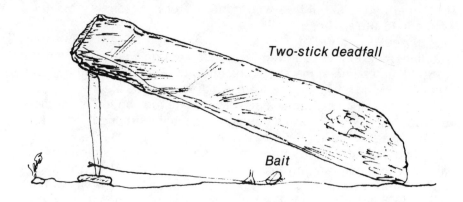

Two-stick deadfall

Bait

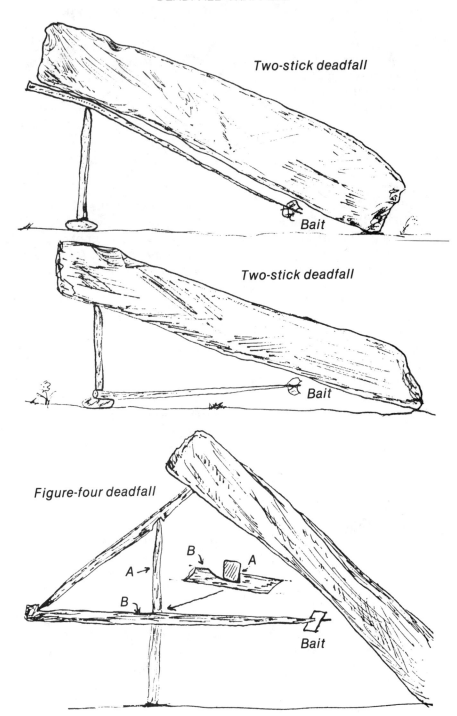

Two-stick deadfall

Bait

Two-stick deadfall

Bait

Figure-four deadfall

B

A

B

A

Bait

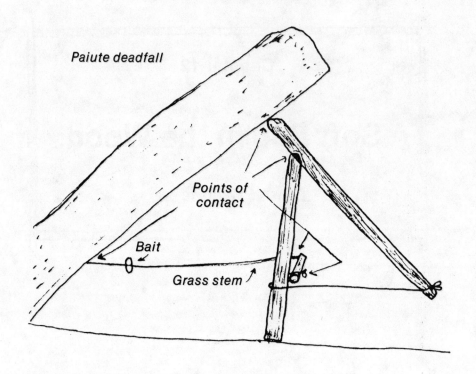

Paiute deadfall

Points of
contact

Bait

Grass stem

Illustrations by Larry D. Olsen

As I look back, there were many things, and many times when, if I had been given the choice, I would not have thought twice about bailing out and/or just giving up completely; and I think had there been none there to pick me up and dust me off, I might have layed there and died. There is a frightening concept in acknowledging this in your character. And yet I never once doubted myself physically. I knew that if I put one foot in front of the other that I could reach or accomplish any goal. This is one of the greatest lessons I have really derived from the (survival) course, which is applicable to just about anything.

Survival Student

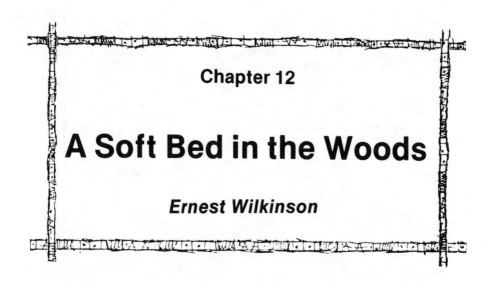

Chapter 12

A Soft Bed in the Woods

Ernest Wilkinson

If you want to enjoy a good night's sleep when you're camping, learn to make your bed from fallen and dried needles from evergreen-type trees. These can be found in abundance under the fir and spruce trees in the mountain areas, and often in fair amounts under the pinon and cedar trees of the drier areas of the lower elevations.

The layers of needles that have accumulated through the years next to the trunks of these trees are usually fairly dry. They can be loosened up with a stick or similar tool and piled onto your poncho or other carriers, then transported a few yards to the intended sleeping area. Spread them out to the desired thickness to form a dry, fluffy mattress under your bed.

These dry needles also make good insulation between you and the damp ground. If there is a half-buried rock or tree root under your chosen sleeping area, you do not have to spend time and energy digging it out or moving in soil to level the spot, which also does some ecological damage when chopping out the sod or other vegetation. Just pile the loose needles around the obstruction to sufficiently cover it.

Or if one end of the chosen sleeping area is lower than the other end, it does not make for a relaxed sleep. Put an old log or some rocks along the lower side to help retain the loose needles. Then pile the dry needles six or eight inches deep on the lower end and perhaps only two inches thick, or whatever level is necessary, on the other end to make the entire area level.

When sleeping out in the winter snows, these dry needles make very good insulation between you and the snow in your snow

Loosen a dry layer of pine needles with a stick or similar tool.

Use dry pine needles to level and insulate beneath your sleeping bag.

Use a log or rows of rocks to corral dry needles for leveling on hillsides.

cave, igloo, or other shelters. Since the winter snows generally slide off the outside boughs of the evergreen trees, the snow is usually shallow next to the tree trunk making it fairly easy to dig it aside to obtain the layer of shed needles.

In the morning, when breaking camp, you can scatter this layer of needles out so the grass or other vegetation can grow up through it; or better yet, gather the layer of needles onto your poncho and redeposit them underneath the tree where you originally found them.

By gathering these evergreen needles and forming them into a mattress of desired thickness for sleeping comfort, you have not disturbed the ecology of the area, nor left an eyesore, as when breaking off evergreen boughs for a bed or digging a level spot as done by many. As more and more folks begin to use the great out-doors for hiking, backpacking, and other types of recreation, I believe it is important that we leave the country behind us as nearly undisturbed as possible for the enjoyment of those following behind us.

Try the use of dried pine needles for your sleeping comfort with no ecological damage to the used area.

Chapter 13

The Stone Axe

Paul Hellweg

Years ago, I used to marvel at how primitive Indians were able to make massive and complex wooden dwellings without the aid of steel axes. Particularly impressive to me was Cahokia, the midwestern Indian city estimated by some accounts to have had a population of 50,000 in the centuries before Columbus. Cahokia was a city which made extensive use of lumber for dwellings, temples, and a protective wall around the city. For a long time the question haunted me: how could such massive projects be undertaken without modern tools?

When I got into survival training, I learned the answer. "Primitive" tools are not really primitive. A properly made stone axe, for example, will readily cut down even the largest tree. Axes of this caliber take considerable time to manufacture—thirty to forty hours not being unreasonable. On the other hand, cruder tools suitable for use in an emergency can be made in an hour or two. This article will cover the spectrum from the crude and quickly made tools to the finely smoothed and polished axes which take so much time to make.

The technique for making axes and hammers is known to anthropologists as "pecked and ground technology." This appears to be an appropriate name because it identifies the two distinctive manufacturing stages involved. The first stage is "pecking" the artifact into rough shape through repeated blows with a hammerstone. Each blow removes minute qualities of material through a crushing or crumbling effect, and the artifact is thus gradually shaped. The second manufacturing stage consists of grinding the artifact into finished form. Grinding is the wearing away of material by abrasion, and is the technique used to put the sharp edge on an axe, celt, or related chopping tool.

The quality of a finished hammer or axe does not depend primarily on manufacturing techniques. Rather, it depends on the degree of hardness of the stone utilized. A coarse stone such as granite can be quickly shaped into a useful hammer, food muller, or related tool. But granite is not suitable for use as an axe. A granite axe could be made in an hour or two for emergency use, but it will not hold an edge and would likely wear out in less time than it took to make. Genuinely efficient chopping tools—the type which can be utilized to fell trees, chop wood, and so forth—must be made from rock much harder than granite. Basalt and andesite are two of the best materials to utilize for quality axes. Tools made from one of these can be resharpened over and over and will last seemingly forever.

Selection of Materials

Selection of a proper stone to use as the raw material, or blank, is thus a matter of importance since it determines the quality of the finished implement. Blank selection also relates directly to manufacturing time. When planning a new axe-making project, I will spend hours looking for the "perfect" blank. My rationale is simple. Five hours spent looking for a good blank is time well spent if it saves ten hours in the manufacturing process. The closer the blank resembles the proposed artifact in size and shape, the less material that will have to be removed in the shaping process. And having less material to remove obviously reduces manufacturing time.

The ideal blank would be a piece of fine-grained, extremely hard rock. These will have a smooth texture and will be comparatively heavy for their size. They must be free of cracks, and thus must be inspected closely. Also, a good blank is homogeneous, that is, of similar consistency throughout. Any change of texture reflects a potential weak spot, and non-homogeneous blanks should be bypassed. Remember, coarser-grained blanks are suitable for hammers, but not for axes.

Of equal importance to the selection of a proper blank is the choosing of a good hammerstone. The pecking hammerstone should be of a rock harder than the stone to be worked, and it too should be homogeneous and free of cracks. Any good hard stone will suffice; however, a siliceous stone of flint, chert, quartzite, or related material would be superior. (Siliceous refers to silicon-bearing rock—in other words, the same type of stone from which arrowheads are made.) The working edge of an ordinary hammer-stone will become blunt with use. In contrast, tiny pieces will flake off a siliceous hammerstone. Instead of dulling, a flint or quartzite hammerstone will continuously resharpen itself during use. In short, any hard rock will work, but a siliceous hammerstone will greatly speed up the pecking process.

Manufacturing Process

Once blank and hammerstones have been selected, the first step in manufacture is to use the hammerstone to peck or pound the blank into the approximate shape of the proposed artifact. The process is simple enough, but some disagreement exists as to the

The first step in the manufacturing of an axe head is rough shaping by peck-ing with a hammerstone of harder material. The hafting groove is pecked as shown, also the blade is rough shaped through pecking.

proper techniques. I can best present the rationale behind my methods by explaining the process through which I came to know them.

I first learned the basics of primitive tool-making as part of my wilderness survival training. A few years later, I was very fortunate in being selected as a participant in Washington State University's summer flint-knapping seminar, co-directed by Jeff Flenniken, WSU's Director of Lithic Technology, and the late Don Crabtree, acknowledged master flintknapper. To these two men, but particularly to Jeff, I owe most of my knowledge of stone tool-making, and I hold both them and their work in deep respect.

I originally learned that the rock being shaped by pecking should not be supported on a hard surface. Instead, I was taught to hold the rock loosely in my hand in order to lessen the danger of its cracking under continuous pounding. But at the WSU field school, Jeff explained that hand-holding was inefficient. The supporting hand "gives" with each hammerstone blow, thus, the blow's force is dissipated and a good portion of the craftsman's effort is wasted. Clearly Jeff was right, and this put me in a bit of a quandary. Experience indicated that if the axe blank is supported on an anvil rock, then it did indeed have a tendency to shatter or crack. Yet having been exposed to Jeff's ideas, I was no longer content to waste time and effort working without support for the piece being worked.

My solution to the support problem is far from profound, but it is practical. The tree stump which I formerly sat on while working has shifted roles. It is now my anvil, and it has proven to be ideal. It offers sufficient support to eliminate wasted effort. More importantly, it is soft enough to give some cushioning and thereby significantly reduce the chances of breaking the rock being shaped. I have done a great deal of work since the field school, and I remain convinced that supporting the blank on a stump, log, or other wood is by far the most efficient method of pecking.

Another area of disagreement which needs to be addressed is whether or not water is beneficial to the pecking process. In theory, at least, it should be. Presumably water would fill the pores of the stone being worked and through a mini-hydraulic effect would transfer the force of each blow over a wider area. However, I remain unconvinced. I attempted an experiment under carefully controlled conditions: weighing twenty specimens to the nearest .01 gram before and after use, recording pecking time, and so forth. My results were inconclusive. Variation from stone to stone (even under identical test conditions) was too great to mean anything. My own opinion, which admittedly is not backed up by incontestable evidence, is that water is of no use for working fine-grained basalt and andesite, and of only limited value for coarser-grained rocks. And that limited benefit is offset by the water's tendency to hold waste material in place and thus obscure the working surface. I find that I get the best results by precisely aiming my hammerstone blows at "high" spots. This I cannot do with the working surface obscured, thus I prefer to work without water. But until more accurate experimental results can be obtained, the use of water appears to be a matter of personal choice.

Axes and Hammerheads

If making a hammer, only a hafting groove need be pecked out. This can be accomplished in as little as a half hour under ideal conditions. For a hammerhead, the hafting groove should be placed at the center of balance.

For axes, on the other hand, the groove should be positioned well aft—at the point where the center of gravity is likely to be after the blade end is thinned and sharpened. Pecking an axehead will take considerably longer than the simple grooving of a hammerhead. This is due in part to the harder nature of a good axe blank. Also, the shaping of an axe is more involved since the blade should also be pecked into its approximate shape prior to grinding.

Rather than trying to imitate a jackhammer, the stone artisan should make his hammerstone blows deliberate and methodical. If a steady rhythm is developed, more work can be accomplished in the long run than can be achieved through brief energetic spurts of activity. Each blow should be moderately hard—light taps are unproductive; heavy pounding risks breaking the stone being shaped. Continue pecking until the hafting groove is cut to desired depth, and the entire tool has been worked into its approximate shape. If making a hammerhead, it is now complete and ready for hafting. But if the artifact is intended as a chopping or cutting tool, one more stage in manufacture is required—grinding the blade to a sharp edge.

Grinding is best accomplished on an abrasive rock, such as sandstone or decomposing granite. Smoother rock can be used for grinding if sand is added as an abrasive. The axe is pressed firmly down, and rubbed back and forth methodically. The grinding slab should be rinsed periodically to cleanse off accumulating waste material. The grinding process is tedious, but no special skill is required until the final shape is almost reached. At this point, grinding becomes more delicate and the artisan must be attentive. As

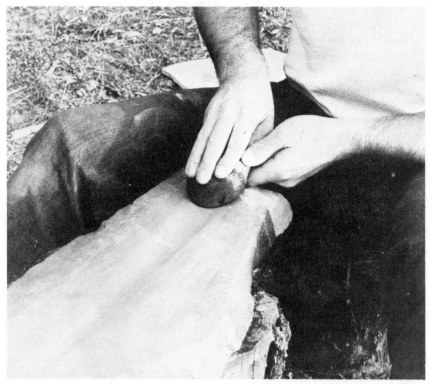

Once the rough shape of the axe head is prepared through pecking, final shape is achieved by grinding. Notice the groove worn in this sandstone grinding slab from many hours use.

the blade nears completion, the final shaping should be accomplished in one direction only—away from the body. If final abrading is done in both directions, then small particles are apt to be broken or pulled off during the backward stroke. Such rough spots cannot be accepted on the cutting edge of a finished axe because they serve as potential footholds for larger breaks when the axe is put to use.

Rough spots will sometimes occur on the blade, even if precautions are taken. When this happens, the edge must be "backed off" beyond the trouble spots. Hold the axe straight down on the grinding slab and abrade until the edge is round and smooth. Then repeat the final shaping process, being extra careful this time.

Once the blade is ground as sharp as possible on the grinding slab, it is time to hone the edge to cutting perfection. This is done in much the same manner as sharpening a knife. In fact, a whetstone

The final step in preparing the axe head is sharpening the blade. A small piece of smooth sandstone is rubbed over the cutting edge at an angle of about 20 degrees (this is done in a manner quite similar to sharpening a steel knife).

may be used if available. If not, select a smooth sandstone pebble and rub the axe bit edgewise with a circular motion. During sharpening, the whetstone or sandstone pebble should be held at about a twenty-degree angle to the axe blade (the same angle used to sharpen a steel knife). Continue until the finished edge is impressively sharp, as determined by feeling with a thumb or finger.

The completed axe ready for hafting. This one is made from basalt, and thus required about 35 hours to manufacture. Axes of coarser rock can be completed in considerably less time.

If desired, the sandstone pebble may also be used to smooth the entire body of the axehead. This adds nothing functionally, but the short time required to smooth and polish the finished tool can be richly rewarding aesthetically. I typically go so far as to smooth out the hafting groove, even though the groove is not visible when the axe is secured in its handle. Be careful here—too much polishing has its drawbacks. It is possible to become enthralled with a finely made implement and then not want to put it to practical use.

Willow-wrap Haft

The final step in construction is hafting; that is, putting on the handle. I have seen quite a few ways to haft axes, but I will limit my discussion here to just two: the willow-wrap handle and the celt-style handle. These are about the two easiest hafts to fabricate, and they both are extremely durable.

I learned of the willow-wrap from Larry Dean Olsen's book, *Outdoor Survival Skills.* A slender willow is selected and heated over the coals of a fire. The willow should be slowly twirled in order to assure uniform heating. When steam is heard escaping, the willow is ready for use. It is now pliable and can be easily wrapped around the hammer or axehead. Hold the axe near the center of the willow and wrap each end completely around the stone. Then quickly secure the willow with leather thongs, rawhide, or any other available cordage. If no cord is available, the haft may be secured with

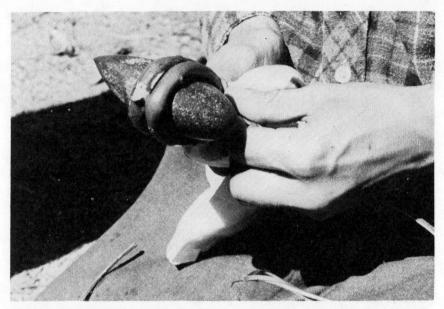

Wrapping a willow handle onto the axe head. The most common error is to use willow too thick for the purpose. Note that this willow is of a thickness about equal to that of the little finger.

young willow shoots, but these too should first be made more pliable by heating over coals.

The willow-wrap handle looks delicate and does not inspire great confidence. In order to satisfy my curiosity, I was determined to find the haft's breaking point. I accordingly took the axe which I had made to illustrate this article (see accompanying photos), and subjected it to excessive abuse. I started chopping on a fallen oak tree, and applied ever increasing force. The handle was obstinate and defied my attempts to break it. Not to be outdone, I took hold of the small axe with both hands, and chopped with all my strength. Nothing. I then had a friend attempt the same experiment. He is bigger and stronger than me, yet he too failed to break the haft. We left feeling frustrated, but impressed by the handle's strength.

We did, however, notice one shortcoming of the willow handle: the slender willow twisted to the side during energetic chopping. The twisting effect somewhat reduced control and made chopping a little awkward. This is a problem that the celt-style handle does not have. The primary advantage of the willow-wrap handle is its ease and quickness to manufacture, important points in an emergency. But if more time is available, I would recommend making a celt instead.

Securing the willow-wrap handle with a leather thong. Willow shoots may also be used, if thongs or other cord is not available.

The finished axe—ready for use!

View of two celts hafted into willow handles. Note how the celt head tapers in, the widest point being at the blade. The celt thus wedges itself more securely into the handle, and the haft becomes stronger with repeated use. (Celt on the left made by Don Fisher. Other tools pictured made by author.)

The Celt Axe Handle

The celt, and its manner of construction, are ideas which I picked up from Jeff Flenniken at the WSU field school. The celt head is made in a wedge-shape, and does not have hafting grooves. It is made thinner and narrower at the butt than at the chopping edge. It is then slipped into a corresponding hole which is carved completely through a handle. The completed celt is the essence of simplicity and ruggedness—the more it is used, the tighter the head is wedged into place.

The handles of the two celts pictured are both made from willow. An average celt handle can be whittled from a branch 2 to 2½ inches in diameter by about 18 inches in length. The bottom is trimmed to a comfortable fit for the hand, but the top should be left large and bulky to provide support for the celt stone. A good handle will take a couple hours to carve, even longer if using primitive carving tools. Once completed, though, the celt makes a durable and effective chopping tool.

The random cutting of trees cannot be condoned. But if a genuine need exists, then a stone celt or hand axe can be of unquestionable value. Wickiup or lodge poles of about two or three inches diameter can be felled in under five minutes. But for felling of larger trees, the survivalist will need either a bigger stone axe or more patience.

A concluding word on the manufacture of stone tools: A friend once remarked that he considered chopping firewood to be highly therapeutic work. I concur wholeheartedly, and would like to add my own comment. Not only is chopping wood rewarding, but the hours spent making the axe can be equally relaxing and rewarding. It all depends on mental attitude. When I settle down to a long pecking or grinding session, I try to work at a steady, rhythmic pace. The effect is much the same as chanting or meditating. In fact, I frequently do chant or meditate in conjunction with the work. Or imagine myself living with an Indian tribe hundreds of years in the past. As of this writing, I have no dream of duplicating the temples of Cahokia. But I am ready should a neighbor need a tree removed.

Photos by Paul Hellweg and Don Fisher.

While on a survival trip with a friend of mine, we were trying to select the best camp area. He wanted one and I the other. The more convinced he became that his was the right choice, the more I knew I was right. It's obvious, of course, that he was being extremely bullheaded, while I, on the other hand, was merely being courageous in my convictions.

Dallan Hendry

I was a little astounded at the energy I had to run up ahead, going up and down mountains to find the trail to Perkins Ranch. It was not physical energy that surprised me, but more a mental energy to push me on. My body was controlled by my mind, and I did not realize this until our forced and exciting march; and as I look over it now, it had been this way the whole time I was out there.

Survival Student

Chapter 14

Primitive Fishing

Richard Jamison

Driving home from town one Sunday afternoon, I passed a fellow decked out in all the paraphernalia of a true angler. He was standing on the road casting into the irrigation ditch—a ditch which had been dry all winter. I imagine this old boy enjoyed the peace and quiet of country fishing and that in itself is often prize enough, but he could have caught more fish in his bathtub.

What I'm getting at is that many people have misconceptions about fishing. They think all they have to do is drop a line in a stream and be patient and sooner or later they will pull out something worthwhile. Not so—fishing is an art, and even under ideal conditions and with the best of equipment, it isn't always productive. (I'd rather not elaborate on the number of times I've been skunked myself.)

Under primitive conditions you are even more handicapped, and you can waste a lot of time and energy trying for that "big one." Don't get me wrong, you "can" catch fish by primitive methods, and there are even occasions when sitting around under a shade tree by a cool water hole, pole in hand, is good therapy. It gives you an opportunity to rest body and soul and still do something worthwhile—the very process which often helps in decision making and productive thinking.

But your main objective should be to catch as many fish as possible with as little effort as possible. This means you will need more than one line in the stream at a time. You may want as many as fifteen or twenty lines, set out in different areas of the stream, if materials permit.

Small bone hooks can be carved and attached with strong fiber cordage.

Hook and Line Fishing

Your first task is going to be securing enough material for several lengths of cordage—good strong cordage that will stand some soaking. Next you will need several hooks. These can be made of bone or wood that has been fire hardened. There are three or four different types of hooks that will be effective, depending on the type and size of fish you are planning to catch. Of course the traditional "J"-shaped hook can be carved from bone or wood and weighted with bait for any type of catch.

To get the most from your effort in a survival situation you would want to fish with a line and several stringers. In other words, you will tie six or seven short lines to the primary one at about two or three-foot intervals. You don't use a pole for this kind of fishing, but attach one end securely to a stake or rock on the bank and let the current of the stream carry the line out in an arc. The best position is on the bend of a stream so the constant movement of the current will keep the line moving. Be sure to weight the line down enough to keep the stringers beneath the water. If the stream is narrow, you may want to attach the primary line to both sides, being sure that you leave enough slack to keep the weighted stringer beneath the water.

Fishing Small Waterways

Small waterways can be damned effectively, so that the water continues to flow but the fish can't pass through. This is best done with rocks stacked in alternating rows. Don't suppose that small streams are not worth fishing. As a matter of fact, they are usually easier to fish, and just as productive as the larger ones. A good example of this was brought home to me while on a fishing trip to northern Wyoming several years ago.

Being an avid fly fisherman, I packed all my gear and hand-tied flies, and we started out for a day of fishing. We drove and drove over winding dirt roads until we came to a canyon with what I would call a "creek" about three feet wide. I was amused, to say the least, and somewhat disappointed that we had driven so far for nothing. Needless to say, I had serious doubts about catching anything of any significance in this so-called stream.

We walked a little way up the canyon to some deeper pockets and my friend suggested that I go first. He said that as I pulled my catch to the bank he would cast in his line—that way we could make the best use of our time. Now I was "sure" he had me on a snipe hunt, but I tossed in my line and as soon as it hit the water a good-sized trout hit the fly. Sure enough, we spent the next hour and a half reeling in pan-sized brookies. I won't say how many we turned loose, but we had more than enough for dinner plus some for the freezer. (In spite of all my fancy hand-tied flies, we caught every single fish on a 5-cent Japanese black gnat.)

The Fish Trap

Another good primitive method of catching fish is the willow fish trap. It is much more simple to build than it looks. You'll need about 60 saplings, approximately 4 to 4½ feet in length, and about as big around as your index finger. I like to leave the bark intact instead of peeling the willow because it looks more natural in the water. When you collect your willow, you will notice that the young shoots growing in the center of the stand are straighter than those growing around the outer edges of the stand. Trim off any branches and cut the willows to the same length.

Place the willow fish trap in the stream positioned in a natural channel.

Willow bark is the fastest, easiest and most available material for twining a fish trap. If you are careful, you can plane off about 6 fairly uniform strips of willow bark from a single stem. The bark needs no further preparation and will remain strong and tight as long as it is kept in the water.

Some people like to make a door that swings inward when the fish enters, then won't swing out, trapping the fish already inside, but allowing more to enter. Personally, I prefer several sharpened "spears" of willow laced into place to keep the fish from swimming out. You will only need about half the number of spears as the total number of willows in the circumference of the trap.

Fish can be kept in a fish trap and used when needed, which is another advantage over the hook, line, and sinker method when you are fishing for survival.

Hopefully I don't need to remind you that this type of fishing is illegal and should only be undertaken in a survival situation. However, now is the best time to build a fish trap, just for the practice, then a good exercise in willpower will come when you fight the urge to use it.

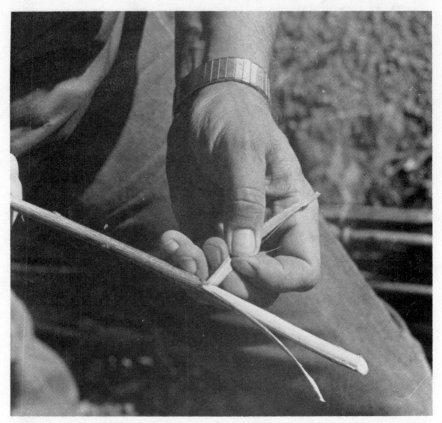

Willow bark can easily be peeled from the stem and used for twining the trap.

Award-winning recipe for cooking suckers: Gut and skin sucker, nail it to a plank torn from the side of an old barn. Using the plank as a reflector for the campfire, cook for at least two hours. Remove fish from the board. Throw fish away and eat the board.

Dallan Hendry

Chapter 15

The Art of Making Arrowheads

Paul Hellweg

A finely made arrowhead can be enchanting. If its proportions are balanced and its flaking is regular, then it truly qualifies as a work of art. Some archaeologists even consider stone tools to be man's first art form. They have found an abundance of stone tools in which the craftsman has gone beyond the mere fabricating of a functional implement. What, then, was early man's motivation to make his tools delicate and proportioned when these qualities did not enhance function? Is it unreasonable to assume that the maker was striving to achieve an ideal of perfection? And if this is not art, what is?

The art of making arrowheads, knives, spear points, and related tools is known as pressure flaking. This is a skill; like any skill, it requires practice to master. I have found that a novice can learn to make functional points in under an hour, assuming he has the correct materials available. But many long hours of practice are required to turn out the finer specimens which could be considered artistic.

In this article, I will present all the fundamentals of pressure flaking. Using these techniques, the beginner can quickly learn to make functional tools—tools which are practical for survival training. I will also discuss more advanced techniques for the benefit of those desiring to perfect their flintknapping (stone working) skills. Regardless of whether the goal is functional tools or museum showpieces, the place to begin is with a look at the necessary materials.

Raw Materials

In technical jargon, minerals suitable for flintknapping are vitreous; that is, they have the near texture of glass. In fact, glass

SAMPLES OF RAW MATERIALS

JASPER   QUARTZ   FLINT   CHERT   CHALCEDONY

MEXICAN   STAINED   PETRIFIED   7-UP   MAHOGANY
GREEN   GLASS   WOOD   BOTTLE OBSIDIAN
OBSIDIAN

A variety of minerals are suitable for making arrowheads. Among the better ones are (top, left to right): jasper, quartz, flint, chert, chalcedony, and (bottom) Mexican obsidian, stained glass, petrified wood, bottle glass, mahogany obsidian. (All arrowheads made by author.)

itself is ideal. It is readily available, and like obsidian (the natural equivalent of glass), it is among the easiest of materials to flake. Fragments of flat window glass would be best, but pieces from any broken bottle will suffice.

The naturally occurring minerals which are suitable for flint-knapping are glass-like in two respects: they contain silicon and they are cryptocrystalline. This latter property means that the mineral's crystal structure is so small that it practically cannot be seen. In essence, the mineral behaves as if it had no crystal structure (as is the case with glass). Glass is technically a fluid in the sense that a force applied to it will spread equally in all directions—much in the same manner that ripples spread outwards on the surface of a pond. It is this ability to transfer force that makes the siliceous minerals suitable for knapping.

When choosing any stone for flintknapping, try to find samples that are as free as possible from impurities and cracks. Some of the above, like flint, are difficult to work. Obsidian, at the other extreme, flakes readily and is the ideal material for the beginner. It occurs naturally throughout the American West, often in prodigious quantities. If none is to be found nearby, then it can be obtained at most rock and gem stores (for a price, of course).

Under no circumstances whatsoever should Indian quarry or campsites be despoiled by an overzealous flintknapper looking for raw material. The waste stone chips at an Indian site tell the archaeologist just as much as finished artifacts. It is thus a crime, both morally and legally, to remove chips from Indian sites. Besides, it is never necessary. If no other material is available, plain old glass works admirably.

Below is a list of the minerals most commonly utilized in the manufacture of flaked stone tools.

Flint
Obsidian
Chalcedony
Chert
Jasper
Agate
Quartzite
Quartz Crystal
Petrified Wood

The Flintknapper's Tools

Next in importance to choice of raw materials is the tools used by the knapper. Indians commonly used pressure flaking tools made from the tips of deer antlers (known as tines). When doing pressure flaking, the tine is used to press small flakes off the stone being worked. Tines are strong enough to do this work, yet their softness allows them to "grip" the stone's edge. This is an important property of antlers. Harder pressure flakers have a tendency to slip—the result is inferior workmanship plus increased danger of cuts to the workman's hands. Antler tines are thus still among the best of tools. If you have trouble locating them, try either a swapmeet, taxidermy shop, or Indian curio store.

Many of today's best flintknappers prefer pressure flakers made from copper wire. Copper has the same hardness/softness characteristics as antlers, but it has the advantage of greater convenience. The copper wire is set in a wood handle which makes a better hand grip; also, the copper does not wear down as quickly as tines.

The best copper pressure flakers are made from heavy-guage wire. Either 2 or 4 gauge hard-drawn wire will work. But hard-drawn wire of this thickness is difficult to find, and it may have to be special-ordered from an electrical supply company. One-inch dowling makes an excellent handle for the wire. Drill a hole endwise, slightly smaller than the wire, then hammer the wire into position, leaving about two

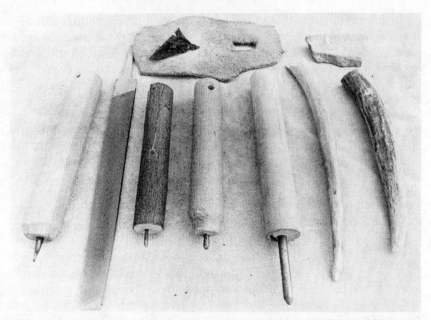

Pictured here are a variety of copper, steel, and antler pressure flakers used to make arrowheads. Also pictured are a sandstone abrading pebble, protective hand pad, and metal file for sharpening copper and steel tools.

inches of copper exposed. Finally, file the wire to a pencil point, and the pressure flaker is ready for use.

Copper wire of the correct size and hardness really is difficult to find. If unavailable, an ordinary nail can be used instead. Drill out the dowling as before, and drive the nail into position. To finish the tool, simply file the exposed head to a workable point. Nails should be used as a last resort, however, since they are hard and have a tendency to slip in use. Slipping can be avoided somewhat by keeping the working point roughened.

If you become seriously interested in making arrowheads, you are likely to accumulate a whole set of pressure flaking tools. My own tool kit includes flakers of antler, copper, and steel—with several sizes of each. A variety of tools gives the worker flexibility. I use my larger implements for general work, and the smaller ones for delicate tasks (such as notching tiny arrowheads). But only one is all you need to get started.

Only two other items are required to start making arrowheads: a sandstone abrader and a leather hand pad. A small sandstone pebble (about 1½ to 2 inches) makes the best abrader, but other coarse pebbles will work if no sandstone is available. The hand pad is best made from thick, but pliable, leather. The pad should be rectangular (about 4 by 6 inches) and needs to have a thumbhole cut in the upper lefthand corner.

Percussion Flaking

The types of workable minerals have already been discussed. But before you can start pressure flaking, these raw materials have to be available in the form of small chips (each chip only slightly larger than the size of the proposed artifact). It should be possible to find chips of the proper size; however, it may be necessary to prepare them yourself. The technique of detaching chips (properly known as flakes) from a rock core is known as percussion flaking. This differs dramatically from the previously mentioned pressure flaking. In pressure flaking, small flakes are pressed off. In percussion flaking, larger flakes are struck off.

In addition to the tools discussed above, you will need the following items to prepare your own flakes: safety goggles, leather gloves, and a fist-sized hammerstone. The gloves and goggles are essential for safety, the hammerstone does the work. Exercise the utmost care in doing percussion flaking—the rock may shatter and send fragments flying (thus the goggles). And if the rock core is held improperly, a finger can be sliced by the flake as it detaches (thus the gloves for hand protection).

Percussion Flaking

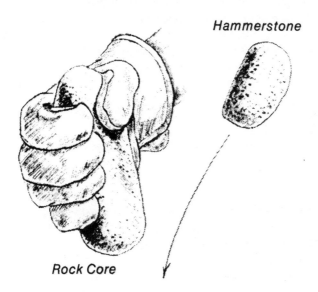

Hammerstone

Rock Core

The technique itself is quite simple: merely strike the rock core with a hammerstone to detach flakes. The hammerstone should be of hard (not crumbly) sandstone, about fist-sized, and with one side flat. Sandstone is ideal—it will detach flakes without shattering the core rock. Harder stones, however, will also work (they are even preferred by some artisans).

Grip the core rock firmly, taking great care to having the fingers well back from the side where the flakes are to be struck. Also be careful of the direction flakes are struck—they sometimes come flying off with considerable force. Swing the hammerstone in an arc, making contact between the *flat* side of the hammerstone and the *edge* of the core rock. Strike at an angle less than a straight-in 90 degrees (about 70 degrees is best). Do not strike straight-in, as this will cause the core to shatter.

Size of the detached flake is determined by two factors: angle and location of the hammerstone blow. The closer the striking angle is to 70 degrees, the larger the resulting flake will be. Lower angle blows produce correspondingly shorter flakes. Strike right at the edge for thin, flat flakes suitable for making arrowheads, but strike a little ways back from the edge for larger flakes. Be careful when trying for larger flakes—this will cause shattering if done improperly.

One rule is useful to keep in mind when doing percussion flaking: follow ridges. Remember that the force spreads equally in all directions. This is true only to the extent that there is sufficient mass to transfer the blow. In practice, the force will spread furthest along ridges on the core rock. Thus, by aligning his blows so that the applied force follows an existing ridge, the skilled flintknapper is able to consistently strike long flakes. This is an advanced technique, however, and is of little practical value to the beginner. If you are a beginner, then you should stick to striking the *edge* of the core with the *flat* side of your hammerstone. By so doing you will be able to strike serviceable flakes almost immediately. But whether attempting beginning or advanced techniques, never forget the safety factors. Wear protective gloves and goggles, strike with caution, and you'll still have all your fingers for next summer's Woodsmoke Rendezvous.

Pressure Flaking

A flake that is ready to be made into an arrowhead is technically known as a blank. Once you have obtained a reasonable supply of blanks, you are ready (finally) to start making arrowheads. This is done by pressure flaking; that is, by pushing off small pieces (pressure flakes) with the pressure flaking tool (antler tine, etc.). Size and

Pressure Flaking

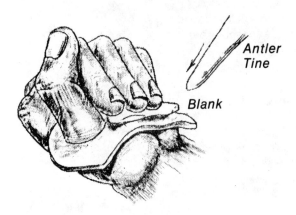

Antler Tine

Blank

shape of the finished point is determined by the location where material is removed. Depending on the size of the original flake and the worker's skill, any number of various artifacts may be made by pressure flaking. Examples include spearheads, arrowpoints, knife blades, fish hooks, hide scrapers, drills, and so forth (see photo).

The original blank is likely to have extremely sharp edges. These should be ground flat in order to lessen the danger of cutting yourself and to provide a better gripping surface for the antler tine. Using the sandstone pebble, grind all edges of the blank. Resist the temptation to blow away the resulting grit; this residual material also improves the antler's grip. If you are using a piece of broken glass or other blank that has a thick edge, refer to the section on alternate flaking (under advanced techniques) for tips on how to get started.

Body position is extremely important to proper pressure flaking. For best results, sit on a low stool, bench, or tree stump. The protective pad goes on your left hand, with the thumb through the hole provided. Position the working blank on your protected palm, and hold the blank securely in place with the fingers. Work with your knees pressed together and with the left hand wedged between your legs. This creates a stable posture with very little danger of the blank accidentally shifting.

Carefully align the antler tine in the direction the small pressure flake is to be removed. Flakes are removed from the bottom of the blank; therefore, align the antler on the bottom portion of the blank's edge. Do not press straight into the blank—this will succeed only in crushing the edge. As in percussion flaking, the force is best applied

Correct body position is important to quality work. The author demonstrates how to hold the blank being worked and the pressure flaking tool. Note that this is a stable position, with both hands well supported.

at a small angle from straight-in (about 85 to 88 degrees). The closer force is applied to this angle, the longer the resulting flake. Pressure is applied inward, with a slight downward "pull" which peels the pressure flake off the bottom of the blank. To do this properly, grip the flaking tool securely in the right hand. Keep the wrist straight and forearm pressed close to the body, thereby eliminating unwanted shifting of the pressure flaker at the moment force is applied.

And that's all there is to it. Really! Pick out some of your poorest blanks for practice. Once you've learned to run some decent pressure flakes, select a better blank and try making an arrowpoint. Do this by selectively removing material to achieve the desired shape of your arrowhead.

The hardest part of making arrowheads is getting the materials together in the first place. Once you've accomplished that, the rest will proceed rapidly. I've found that the average student is able to make decent arrowpoints after an hour or less of instruction. It might take longer without instruction, but you'll probably still be surprised at how quickly you learn. When getting started, do not confuse yourself by moving on to the advanced techniques too rapidly.

Advanced Techniques

I'll be discussing three advanced techniques: alternate flaking, platform preparation, and ridge alignment. As already mentioned, the first is a method for getting started on blanks with thick edges. The later two are used by skilled artisans to run long uniform pressure flakes. If you want to make "brag" pieces to show off to your friends, then these are the skills to master.

Alternate Flaking: Normal pressure flaking is next to impossible on blanks with thick square edges. These troublesome edges are best removed by alternate flaking; that is by removing pressure flakes from alternate sides. Start at one corner and remove a short stubby flake by changing the angle of the antler tine to about 45 degrees. Then flip the blank over and remove a similar short stubby flake from the opposite side. For this second flake, do not position the tine on the blank's original edge. Instead, start the second flake from the new edge created by removing the first flake. Continue in this manner until the entire thick edge is removed. Each time, flip the blank over and start from the newly exposed edge left by the previous effort. Once the entire edge is removed, then the rest of the blank may be worked by standard pressure flaking techniques.

Platform Preparation: In order to run long pressure flakes, the antler must be positioned on a well-defined platform. Use the sandstone abrading pebble to prepare this platform. Holding the blank firmly, roughly abrade in *one direction* only. Then turn the blank over and run your pressure flakes in the *opposite direction.* This rough

Alternate Flaking

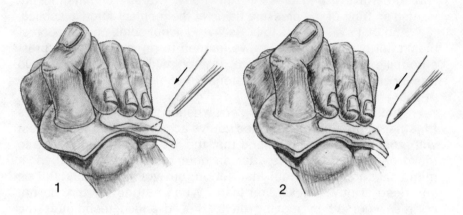

Platform Preparation

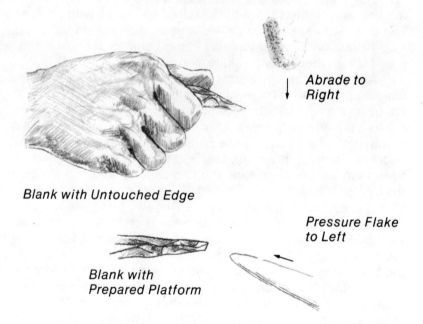

Blank with Untouched Edge

Abrade to Right

Blank with
Prepared Platform

*Pressure Flake
to Left*

abrading in the opposite direction establishes the clearly defined platform which is necessary for long pressure flakes.

Ridge Alignment: The section on percussion flaking discussed how the force of a blow travels furthest along existing ridges. The same is equally true of pressure flaking. If the antler tine is positioned such that force is applied in the direction of a ridge, then longer pressure flakes can be achieved. The skilled artisan thus utilizes the ridge left behind by the preceeding pressure flake. You can do this too by carefully positioning the antler tine for each effort. Whatever the width of the previous flake, move the tine about half that distance for the next. This then aligns the center of the new flake over the ridge left behind by the previous flake. By continuing in this manner, each pressure flake will have a ridge to follow. This is a difficult technique to master, but if you practice hard you will eventually be able to run long parallel pressure flakes. And then you'll be creating works of art—works that we'll all be waiting to see at the next Rendezvous.

A variety of artifacts may be made utilizing the techniques discussed. Pictured here are a fish hook, four arrowheads (one at each corner), knife blade (center row, left to right), awl, spear point, drill, and atl-atl dart point. For reference, the spearhead is 6 inches long. (All artifacts made by author.)

Acknowledgments

I wish to thank Mark West and Mike Seacord for their assistance in preparing this article. Mark is a professional photo-journalist, and he has prepared all of the accompanying photographs. The drawings are by Mike Seacord. Mike is an archaeologist working with the National Park Service, and he is also a skilled flintknapper.

I am also indebted to Jeff Flenniken and the late Don Crabtree. Most of what I know about this art was learned at Washington State University's flintknapping field school, which was co-directed by these two men. Jeff is likely the best flintknapper working today, and Don pioneered most of the techniques presented in this article.

I found some muddy water, a runoff of some melting snow along the roadway. I knew I shouldn't drink it, but did anyway. This didn't help my situation for I became sick also. I remember that I felt really bad and did mention this, but I never complained that I couldn't continue—I wouldn't let myself do that. I knew then that if I let an excuse get me out of something I didn't feel up to, I would look for an excuse every time.

From this one rather unpleasant situation, I gained something of importance—I had reversed a trend. Before I was able, if things went wrong, to just turn my back on a problem. But that day, I stood and finished what I started. I felt good about it. I think that day was the hardest day for me, yet I finished what I started.

Survival Student

On survival there can be no falling behind in the search for food. The same application of efforts should be present in my own conquest of everyday home, school, and life ideals. I must discipline myself to keep up my pace in my challenges and, if I do get behind, to quicken my step so I can achieve those ideals I have set out to attain. I know now more of and about my own potential and that it increases with my will and endeavors to reach my goal. I know of my potential not because I think I can climb a mountain myself, but I know it because I have done it.

Survival Student

Chapter 16

Troubleshooting: Bow and Drill Fires

Richard Jamison

There are several methods of fire-starting using natural materials. Your success is utilizing them will depend largely on the quality of your materials and your experience, or the quality of instruction you receive.

Having tried many different methods, it seems that for ease and time invested (it takes more arm strength for other methods), the bow-drill is the most practical. This doesn't mean that other techniques don't work—they do, and you may prefer the hand-drill or fire plow simply because it works well for you. That's fine—just remember that it is always best to have a back-up system in the event you run into trouble with your old stand-by.

Building fires with a bow and drill is exciting. Your self-confidence will increase, just knowing that you have produced flame from what nature has provided. The bow and drill can also be a *fast* way to start fires. In fact, it isn't uncommon to have a flame in less than 60 seconds when done properly—if, of course, you already have your materials collected and prepared. It is also a beautiful skill to observe.

But sometimes a 60-second fire just isn't in the picture (especially when you are demonstrating the technique before a large group). Even the most experienced outdoorsman will have problems pop up. Sometimes the only warmth you will generate is body heat exerted from trying to start the fire, rather than from the crackling of flames.

By experimenting with different kinds of wood, it appears that there could be different combinations of trouble. Our experiments of one day produced over 35 fires made with various combinations of wood. Later experiments also included varied weather conditions, from wind and rain to snow and below-freezing temperatures. The ultimate victory was 100% success with 15 students in conditions of -10 degrees with a 20 mph wind, while being photographed for a newspaper article!

Many times during the course of a workshop, 100% of the participants have success with the bow and drill method, while at other times the individual may work independently for weeks, and even months, only to find one little "trick" once learned will give him or her immediate success.

Selection of Materials

First, the proper selection of materials is necessary. Different sections of the country will, of course, have varying materials available. For instance, yucca is available and very abundant in the southwestern part of the United States, but not in the north. Basswood is available in the northeast, but not in the south and west, etc. You will need to locate the proper materials in your own locale.

Soft-woods work best, such as yucca, willow, aspen, birch, basswood and cottonwood. The various pines are soft woods, but too resinous to be of use for friction-fire methods.

Select your woods from broken branches that are found above ground. Wood that has been lying on the ground for several years absorbs too much moisture, and tends to be rotten. Dead branches that are found in the trees are more likely to be dry than those on the ground.

Preparing the Materials

There are four basic parts to a bow-drill set. The drill, the socket, a fireboard, and a bow. Begin by cutting a *drill*. It is made of a piece of wood 7 to 10 inches long, and about ½ to ¾-inch in diameter. It should be as straight as possible. If it has any knots or rough places, whittle them off until it is smooth. This is very important, so that the drill will spin smoothly.

One end of the drill is rounded off, while the other is sharpened so it will turn freely in the socket. The blunt end creates friction on the fireboard.

The *fireboard* is made from a longer piece of wood and should be whittled down to about ½-inch thick, 2 inches wide, and about 7 to 8 inches long. A smaller piece can be used, but the extra width will allow you to start many fires on both sides of the fireboard.

The *socket* is used to allow the drill, or spindle, to turn freely in the palm of the hand. The best material is a rock with a small

Find a flat, smooth stone and make a depression for the drill to turn in.

depression. A piece of bone or hard wood will work also, but stone is preferable. The depression always seems to stump our students. They spend hours working to get a dent in the stone. The secret is to find a rock that is soft enough to work, yet not too abrasive to wear the drill down too fast. You probably have one blade on your knife that you use for utility, as a tool. Use it to notch out the depression, or a sharp stone can be used to chip it. Wet the stone while you drill.

The next item is the *bow*. It should be of green, flexible material. A straight piece of willow about ¾ of an inch in diameter and about 2½ feet long is ideal. In fact, a longer bow is preferable to insure better rhythm. If the bow has a "y" on one end, the cordage may be attached more easily. The opposite end of the bow should have a notch cut around the willow to hold the cordage. It might be mentioned here that the cordage should never be cut—it is too valuable an asset to have it cut in short pieces. Just wrap the excess around the "y" end of the bow and tie it off.

The *bow string* can be made from any strong piece of cordage such as leather strips, parachute cord, shoe laces, or strips cut from a leather belt. Strong natural cordage will work well also, especially that made from dogbane.

Once all the materials are collected for the bow and drill set, you will need to collect fire material. There are several types necessary: tinder, kindling and fuel. Many times the material collected for tinder is too large to ignite and burn quickly. Dry grass, cattail or milkweed down, plant fiber, or the inner bark of dead trees are all recommended tinder material. Proper preparation of the tinder is also extremely important to the success of fire-building. If the tinder is coarse, it should be twisted and rubbed until it becomes soft and downy.

Everything must be absolutely dry. This is the reason you use the "inner" bark of trees. The pith from various plants such as mullein, milkweed, dogbane or sunflower will also ignite readily and can be used as tinder. Additional good tinder material includes dry fiber from any plant, and down from the seed pods of cattail, thistle, milkweed, clematis, alder or cottonwood. The dry tinder should be formed into a small "bird's nest" about the size of a tennis ball, and a small depression should be made in the center for the smoldering coal.

The *fireboard* is prepared by cutting a small depression about ¼ to ½ of an inch from the edge. The purpose for the depression is to keep the drill from slipping off the fireboard. Place the fireboard flat on the ground, with no air space beneath. If the ground is wet or damp it will pull the heat from the fireboard during the spinning of the drill, so it is necessary to use some type of dry material beneath the fireboard and the ground if it is damp.

Technique

The following instruction is related to a right-handed person; if you are left-handed, just reverse the technique:

● The sharpened end of the drill must be lubricated. This can be achieved by rubbing it against the scalp to collect oils. Oil can also be collected on the forehead near the hairline or at the side of the nose. Wax from your ears also works well as a lubricant.

● The left foot is placed at the side of the fireboard.

● The blunt end of the drill is down, the sharpened end fits into the socket.

● The cord is wrapped once around the drill and the blunt end of the drill is placed into the depression of the fireboard and held in place with the socket in the left hand.

● *The position of your body is very important* to enable you to apply correct pressure and attain proper balance and smooth action.

Make a slight indentation on the fireboard so that the drill won't slip out as you begin spinning.

Twist the string around the bow one time. Be sure it isn't too loose.

Position of the body is extremely important. The shoulder and drill should form a direct line.

The drill, hand and shoulder must form a straight line, or when the spinning begins the drill will flip out of the depression in the fireboard. The wrist of the left hand is locked in and held firmly against the shin. Be sure that the right knee isn't too close. Some people are too tight—they place their knee too close, causing tension in muscles, and they will tire more easily. This may sound very formal, but once the proper position and technique are learned, the success ratio will climb drastically.

● The end of the bow is grasped in the right hand, the thumb placed between the bow and the cordage to act as a lever to apply tension.

● The bow action must be smooth and even. Long strokes will spin the drill without over-tiring you. Practice until you master a comfortable rhythm. Remember, tension may be applied as needed to the cord, using the right thumb for leverage.

● The tip of the bow should be slanted slightly downward. This will keep the cord from working its way up on the drill.

● At first very little pressure is applied to the drill. Pressure should be increased gradually until the depression in the fireboard is blackened.

Next comes the most important part of the process:

● Using your knife, cut a notch on the underside of the fireboard beneath the blackened depression. The ember will fall through this notch so the edges must be smooth to allow the ember to collect freely.

● Beneath the notch, a small pocket is cut to trap the heat and allow the powder which forms the coal to collect. This is a big problem area—if you have smoke but no spark, check the powder and see if it is black. If it is not black, a faster spinning action is needed,

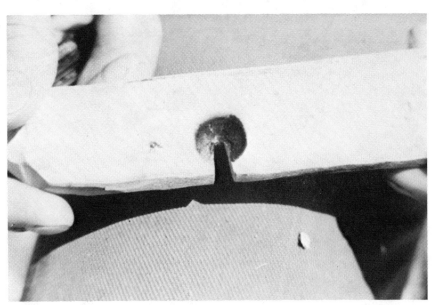

A notch is cut beneath the blackened area of the fireboard. The sides are beveled to allow the coal to drop onto the tray.

Bevel the notch on the underside of the fireboard. This is an important feature often overlooked in the preparation stages.

Place the tray beneath the fireboard to catch the coal.

The spinning is continued using a smooth action until the coal builds up in the notch.

or more pressure. If it still doesn't work, (1) the board and drill may be damp, (2) the notch may not be cut back far enough, or (3) the notch may not be wide enough to allow the spark to fall into the pocket.

● A tray must be placed beneath the notch to catch the ember or coal. This can be a piece of wood shaving, a green leaf, or any other material that can be used to lift the ember to the tinder bundle. Be sure that your tray has not collected dew or moisture—this will only cause the coal to burn out.

Careful Handling and Perseverance

At this point, the only useful advice that can be given is "persevere." Eventually powder will build up in the pocket and the resulting friction heat will create a coal. You will know the coal is burning when you see a faint whiff of smoke coming from the pocket. Continue spinning the bow for an additional 30 seconds, even though you may feel like your arm will fall off at any minute. This will insure a large enough ember that it will not die out before it is transferred to the tinder bundle.

● Now *carefully* remove the spindle and slowly lift the fireboard from the tray. The ember should be on the tray. If it is wedged in the notch, a slight tap on the fireboard should dislodge it. Again, using

Lift the coal into the nest with the tray.

care, transfer the ember into the hole of the tinder bundle. Tighten the bundle around the coal. Blow the ember gently and steadily until it bursts into flame. It may be necessary to squeeze the bundle tighter around the coal, but remember that as long as the coal is still burning, patience will eventually produce flame.

● Place the burning tinder bundle on the ground and build up the fire with small kindling, then add fuel in the standard method.

Once you have learned the "proper" method of making a bow-drill fire, and feel confident and comfortable with it, you can devise shortcuts and your own "tricks" toward that 60-second goal! In one class there was an individual who never seemed able to get a coal, then he noticed that his drill was glowing like a punk. He blew on it until it was hot enough to light his "bird's nest" tinder bundle and had fire. It was not exactly the prescribed method, but whatever works is fair.

A bow and drill fire is most valuable in an emergency situation because none of the materials are commercially manufactured. It is also valuable in building self-confidence, for the individual learns to work with nature and not against her.

The nest is squeezed around the coal and gently blown into flame.

Bow-Drill Fire Troubleshooter's Chart

Fireboard will not blacken:
- a) not enough pressure
- b) damp wood
- c) wood too hard

Spindle flips out:
- a) drill not straight
- b) bow not being held in a straight angle when spun
- c) hole in socket not deep enough
- d) depression in fireboard not deep enough
- e) fireboard not setting level

Spindle wears down quickly:
   a) wood too soft
   b) socket too abrasive

Spindle will not spin:
   a) too much pressure
   b) not enough tension on bow string
   c) drill not straight

Smoke but no coal:
   a) notch not cut deep enough into center of blackened area
   b) ground damp
   c) wood damp
   d) notch not wide enough
   e) stopped too soon

When a person wishes to get to the top of a mountain, he begins to climb from the bottom and works his way upward one step at a time. And if he hikes long enough in an upward direction, he is going to reach the top. A very simple point. Perhaps so simple that I didn't really understand it until I'd been able to climb a few mountains myself.

Survival Student

Chapter 17

A Primitive
Hand Fire-Drill

Ron "Gus" Gustaveson

Man has had acquaintance with fire since the beginning of time. It is not known how fire was first discovered. Man early learned that by twirling one slender piece of wood between the palms of the hands, he could quickly burn or bore a hole through other wood, which was used to be fashioned into implements. It could have been by pure accident that fire was first kindled in this manner. Vague as history is as to how the invention of fire was first discovered, we can be fairly certain that the hand-drill technique is one of the most ancient methods. It has been in constant use by primitive peoples throughout many parts of the globe (wherever the proper selection of wood could easily be appropriated).

Collecting Materials

The hand drill consists of four parts: spindle, fireboard, firepan, and tinder bundle.

● The *spindle* must be a fairly straight, round, slender rod about ½ to ¾ of an inch in diameter and about 18 inches long—the longer the better. When the spindle is in operation, the thickest end should be the one which spins against the fireboard. It is the same end that should be whittled to about ¼ of an inch diameter, back a full two inches from the friction end, and the tip should be blunt. The reason for this reduction in size is to concentrate all friction into one area.

● Your *fireboard* should have a diameter at least a little larger than the spindle (before its end was reduced in size). The fireboard need only be long enough to be held down securely with the foot while the spindle is being twirled. A 5- or 6-inch length is excellent.

● The *firepan* is merely a flat piece of wood or bark onto which the wood dust falls as it is ground out by friction.

● A *tinder bundle* can be made from dry fibers, such as the shredded bark of the juniper, sagebrush, cedar, etc., which has been rubbed between the hands to render it fluffy, and arranged into the approximate contour of a bird's nest. The finer fibers should be in the center.

You should make a small indentation into your fireboard about ¼ inch from either edge, just large enough to admit the spindle's tip, to prevent it from slipping out during the twirling process. The firepan is placed under the fireboard directly beneath this indentation.

A small vertical notch is cut into the blackened depression. As the spindle is turned it allows the wood dust to build up in the notch.

Turn the spindle rapidly between the palms, while bearing down with slight pressure.

The exciting climax comes when the small ember is dumped into the tinder bundle and blown into flame.

Mastering the Technique

If you will either get down on one knee or squat, it will become apparent how easily the fireboard can be held firmly to the ground with the other foot. With the spindle's tip resting in the indentation and held in the vertical position, shift your weight until you feel well balanced and comfortable.

You are now ready to kindle a fire as your primeval ancestors did long ago. The hands are placed at the top of the spindle and the apparatus is rapidly spun between the palms while simultaneously bearing down with a slight pressure. The hands will slowly slip down the spindle. You must quickly re-grasp it at the top and repeat the aforementioned motions.

After a thin wisp of smoke has begun to rise, lift the spindle and you will have enlarged the now slightly blackened depression on your fireboard. A small vertical notch is cut into the side of this to the center of the hole to allow the wood dust to rub out. As soon as the spindle has been replaced into the depression and the afore-mentioned process of twirling has been reverted to, the hands should bear down firmly, gradually increasing in momentum. As smoke again begins to spiral up, bear down and twirl with all of your might until the smoke rises and continues to curl from the small pile of wood dust, which will then have been produced by friction prior to falling through the notch. This small heap is fanned with the hand. The apparatus is now whisked away and the small glowing mass is lifted with the firepan, upon which it has fallen, dumped into your tinder bundle, and quickly blown into flames.

Helpful Hints

Select your fireboard and spindle of well-seasoned wood which has a low ignition point. Yucca is very good for this. The aborigines of Australia use the flower stem of the grass-tree.

Warm wood works best. It is sometimes possible to place your apparatus in the sunlight for a few moments previous to using.

Chapter 18

A Deer is More Than Venison on the Table

Jim Riggs

Each year as the hunting seasons for antelope, bighorn sheep, deer and elk come along, I am reminded of the contrast between the orientation of the modern hunter and his aboriginal counterpart. While the desire to bring home fresh, wild meat remains basic to the hunting incentive, the means, and the hunter's understanding of the natural environment and the game he seeks, seem to have changed considerably.

A modern hunting excursion into the outdoors is a welcome and enjoyable respite from the workaday world, but too often the technological, recreational and "convenience" aspects (four-wheel drives, campers, portable televisions, high-powered scopes and rifles, ad infinitum) subtly retard the progress and intensity of the natural experience. Most peoples' everyday lives are so far removed from the natural cycles of life that hunting trips take them into alien environments. Their experience there seldom lasts long enough for the alienation to grow into familiarity and understanding.

The Modern Hunting Ethic

I think it is man's desire, perhaps unrealized need, that drives him to the hunt, but his lack of knowledge and commitment ultimately lessen that experience and lock him into his alien role. This opinion is reaffirmed whenever I come across a dead deer, one that was shot but evidently ran a ways before falling, and I must conclude that the hunter did not have the patience, skill nor responsibility to track the animal to its final resting place. In rugged country it is not unusual to find an elk carcass with only the hindquarters and backstraps taken—too much hassle to return for a second or third load, I guess.

When I acquire deer hides from hunters and flesh them in preparation for making buckskin, I am continually amazed at the large sheets and hunks of once-superb meat they've left adhering to the skins. Most hides I process are improperly skinned and have two to five or more pounds of meat still attached. It's absurd! The modern way seems to be one of carelessly slashing the skin off sheerly for the thrill of wielding a new knife. A skin is more efficiently and nearly as expediently removed by "fisting" it off—that is, by separating the connective tissue between skin and carcass by hand, after making only a few initial incisions with a knife.

Perhaps the worst of these situations involves a minority of those who hunt, but they occur frequently and do not speak well for the health and evolution of a modern hunting ethic. In these situations it is not so much the waste of meat that bothers me, for the carrion-eaters—the coyotes, vultures, skunks, beetles, yellow-jackets and the like—will devour most of the carcasses. What they leave will gradually return to the soil as part of the organic process. What leaves me scratching my head in wonder is man's attitude and his uncompleted responsibility to the natural cycles of life.

It's not unusual to find a carcass with only the hind quarters and backstrap gone.

Respect for the Prey

The hunting of big game in aboriginal times and hunting today by those who live closely with nature, or have at least once experienced that lifeway, presents quite a different picture. Hunting was not recreation or sport, but a necessary and integral component of existence. It is logical to assume that the challenge of the hunt was enjoyed, that the continual application and testing of one's cummulative knowledge and skills was stimulating, but the reasons for hunting were deeply rooted in sincere need for the animal's meat, hide and additional byproducts. Hunting was directly a life-supporting activity.

While hunting supplied the aboriginal diet with protein and nutrition not steadily obtainable from other food sources, it is interesting to note that in none of the Pacific Northwestern native cultures was hunting the dominant food-providing economic activity. On the coast, fishing and shellfish gathering dominated. Along the Columbia River and its tributaries draining the plateau regions of Washington, Oregon and Idaho, salmon and roots comprised the food staples. In the arid Great Basin between the Sierras and Rockies, about two-thirds of the diet was comprised of vegetable foods, mostly seeds. Whole technologies and implements were developed for the harvesting and processing of seeds, some individually smaller than a pinhead, but lucrative because they could be collected in great quantities. West of the Cascades, economic activities were about equally represented by plant gathering, fishing and hunting.

The importance of specific big game animals varied greatly from one region and culture to another. The Eskimo hunted mainly sea mammals, natives of the tundra and boreal forest the caribou, Great Plains horsemen the bison. In the Great Basin, due to the paucity of larger game, the jackrabbit dominated. But the deer was indigenous to nearly all of North America and is still the most frequently and consistently hunted big game. It is the aboriginal's conception of the deer that sets him apart from the modern hunter.

Because the deer was the source of so many important materials to native cultures, each hunter well understood his prey; he killed the deer, but he appreciated all that it gave him. Before the hunt he often fasted and took a sweatbath to cleanse his mind and body, to pray for success, and to properly attune his attitude and energies. He thanked the deer and the Great Spirit for helping to fulfill his needs. These were not cursory utterances or affectations— "corny" by modern attitudes—these were genuinely expressed feelings, from people who had grown their entire lives knowing and depending on nature, intimately enough to realize that nothing should be taken for granted, that mental attitudes do influence seemingly secular cause-effect relationships. To teach respect, humility and generosity, in many native cultures, it was customary for a boy not to partake of his first deer, but to distribute it among his family, relatives and friends.

Aboriginal cultures, though all materially based on available natural resources, varied considerably due to differing origins and adaptations to widely differing environments. All of these peoples obviously did not utilize all parts of all deer killed, but their knowledge of how they could, when needed, make use of nearly the entire animal is truly amazing. I believe that most modern hunters are further separated from their natural environment and their prey because they lack the familiarity that grows from, and is based on, this "need to use" concept. The uses for a deer described here have been collected from many sources, and it is unlikely that any single aboriginal group was familiar with them all. Most uses apply to other hoofed big game as well as the deer.

Aboriginal hunters may have procured deer with bow and arrow, the atlatl (spearthrower) and dart, tough rawhide or plant fiber snares, via pitfall traps, coordinated drives into enclosures or over cliffs, or numerous other methods. A freshly killed deer was first eviscerated, then cleanly skinned.

Use of the Deer Skin

Sometimes the head skin was removed whole, stuffed with dry leaves or grasses so it would hold its natural shape as it dried, and later used as a hunting decoy. Other times the head skin was left attached so the whole skin could be draped over a hunter with the stuffed deer head resting on top of the hunter's own head for use as effective camouflage in stalking more game. These decoy methods were extremely effective, but a hunter would be taking his life rather lightly if he tried this in the ballyhoo of a modern hunting season!

In the Great Basin where large game was at a premium, the people developed some ingenious uses for normally marginal parts of the skin. "Hock" moccasins were made from the skin encompassing the heel area—about mid-leg—of each of the deer's hind legs. These tubular sections of skin were girdled above and below the hocks, then peeled off like socks; they were naturally shaped to fit small human feet. Modification consisted only of sewing closed the lower end of the skin tube to form the toe portion of each moccasin and adding a couple of skin ties to the upper part so it could

*Jim Riggs with nicely tied stretched mule deer hide drying in preparation
for dehairing as part of buckskin process.*

be bound around the wearer's ankle. The skin was seldom tanned
for these quickly constructed moccasins, and they were often
finished inside out, hair side against the wearer's foot for added
warmth. In the Canadian north, mukluks from moose hocks are
still occasionally made this same way.

Another "quickie" moccasin, termed the Fremont style for the early culture in Utah where it was first found and described, used all four lower leg skins from a deer or bighorn sheep. These untanned pieces of skin were cleverly cut and sewed together so that the dewclaws attached to the skins served as hobnails or grips, four on the sole of each moccasin. One animal's leg skins yielded one pair of moccasins. Nowadays, the lower legs are cut from the carcass and discarded, but an enterprising native could make a pair of hock or Fremont moccasins and still have the rest of the hide to tan for clothing.

The fresh hide was either tanned immediately or stretched out and dried. It could then be kept indefinitely for later tanning, or used untanned. Untanned skins with the hair left on were used for mats and bedding. Eventually, these became fairly soft from use, and by the time most of the hair had broken or worn off, they were made into moccasins or other articles of rawhide, or tanned as buckskin.

Rawhide

Rawhide was prepared and used with varying degrees of refinement. Most simply a skin was soaked in water or buried in the ground for a few days until the hair slipped off easily. Strips cut from a hide prepared in this way were especially useful for sturdily binding things together, because rawhide stretches when wet and shrinks tightly while drying. Larger pieces were used for drum heads. For moccasin soles, quivers, knife and bow sheaths, saddlebags and storage containers, rawhide was further processed. The hair and epidermal layer of skin were scraped from a stretched, dried hide, which was then thoroughly and systematically pounded with round stones to make it thicker and more pliable. Most often, hides heavier than deer were prepared in this way.

Buckskin

Deer hides were usually made into buckskin. The hair and epidermal layer were removed by either wet or dry scraping and the tough, tightly adhering connective tissue scraped from the flesh side of a skin. The hide was then soaked for a few minutes up to a day in an emulsion of the deer's brain mixed with water. Sometimes the brain was mashed and beaten into a paste which was rubbed into the skin. After braining, the skin was wrung out to eliminate all excess moisture, then worked continually by hand or laced onto a square pole frame and worked with oar-shaped sticks until thoroughly dry, soft and pure white. Lastly, if intended for everyday wear

Buckskin moccasins made by students in a Malheur Field Station Aboriginal Life Styles Course. They tanned the deer hides first as part of the course.

and use, the white buckskin was sown into a bag shape and suspended over a smudge fire, first one side, then the other, until it turned the desired shade of yellow, tan or brown. The color depended on the length of time it was smoked and the type of vegetation used to create the smoke. Smoking helped preserve the skin, gave it a pleasing aroma, and allowed it to dry soft after getting wet or being washed.

This basic process, with many variations from one culture to another, produced what we call Indian-tan or smoke and brain-tan buckskin—the soft, warm, strong and durable material many tribes used for their clothing, decorative bags, cradleboard coverings, etc.—almost anything we use cloth or leather for these days.

If the brains were not to be used immediately for tanning, they were lightly boiled and spread to dry in the sun, mixed with dried moss and further dried or sealed in a length of intestine so they would keep until needed. They also could be eaten.

Deer skins with the hair left on could be tanned soft for robes and blankets, but these were hardly worth the hard work of tanning because deer hair, unlike that of furbearing animals, is hollow and brittle and continually breaks and sheds.

Use of the Tail, Ears, Feet and Eyes

The deer's tail was either left on the skin or removed and used for a decoration. The ears could be carefully skinned out, inflated like a balloon and dried in that shape; then, with the insertion of a few pebbles or tiny foot bones from the deer, re-bound closed around a stick handle and used for a ceremonial rattle. From a buck the scrotal skin was softened and fashioned into a naturally shaped small utility pouch.

The whole feet, hooves included, could be coarsely chopped up and boiled to extract the valuable oil which rose to the surface of the water and could be scooped off with a small container. One deer's feet yielded only about a tablespoonful of oil, so this process was usually done only when many feet could be boiled together. This neatsfoot-like oil is an excellent dressing for skins—it was sometimes added to the brain emulsion for tanning buckskins—and was used to condition and preserve antler, bone and wooden tools.

Even the deer's eyes had a special use. The fluid inside them was a medium for mixing with powdered earth pigments, such as red ochre to make paint.

Before a skinned deer was cut up, the hunter removed the all-important sinew. Sinew is a term for the tendons. Leg tendons are rounded in cross section, encased in a tough outer covering and must be pounded with smooth stones or soaked and split open to expose the soft, tough inner fibers. The Achilles tendon in your own heel is a good example of this type of sinew.

Other sinew from the shoulder, back and rump shows as thin, shiny sheets on the surface of the meat. The longest sinew in a deer extends in two flat sheets, each about two inches wide, from the shoulder blades to the pelvis along each side of the backbone. For removal, it must be severed at each end where it narrows and peeled from the backstrap (tenderloin) meat to which it adheres. A fingernail easily separates this naturally striated flat sinew into thin fibers. Sinews were scraped clean and dried for later use.

In aboriginal times, finely shredded sinew fibers served as strong sewing thread, binding material for stone points and feathers on arrows and any other bindings calling for something finer than rawhide. Sinew was the strongest natural material available for twisting into bow strings and snares, and bundles or strips of shredded sinew were affixed to the backs of wooden bows with glue made of boiled fish skin, boiled deer or other mammal skin. Sinew-backed bows were not more powerful, but were more elastic and kept the wood from shattering. Like rawhide, sinew fibers were moistened, usually in the mouth, before application, and they shrank and tightened as they dried.

Meat on the Table

The meat provided by the deer was the main reason the animal was sought, and could be prepared in many ways. Usually the heart, liver, tongue, and occasionally lungs and kidneys were eaten first, as they were not easily preserved. Some portions of meat were eaten raw, or simply thrust onto sticks and roasted over the fire. As the longbones were picked clean of meat, they were cracked open with stones and the nutritious marrow sucked out.

Boiled meat was a favorite. Lacking containers that could be placed directly over a fire, the Northwest cultures developed other ways for boiling foods. Many fist-size or smaller, rounded stones were gathered and placed in a fire until they became red-hot. Then, with wooden tongs, they were dropped into watertight wooden boxes, carved wooden or stone bowls, or tightly woven baskets with the meat and water. More hot stones were added, stirred, and the cooled ones removed until the water had boiled the meat the desired length of time.

Although men on a hunt lacked these kinds of containers so common around the permanent camps, they still invented ways to boil meat. Sometimes they propped the ribcage open, filled it with as much water and meat as it would hold, and proceeded with the same stone-boiling process. Another method was to scoop out a bowl-shaped depression in the ground and line it with a portion of the hide or the opened stomach to serve as the boiling container. Sometimes the boiling was accomplished in the opened stomach, draped bag-like from three or four upright sticks set into the ground. The contents of the stomach were often boiled along with the added meat and then the stomach itself, now thoroughly cooked, was also eaten—a perhaps not-so-tidy feast which, nevertheless, left no dirty dishes!

To preserve meat, make it lightweight and easy to carry, it was sliced into thin sheets or long strips and dried in the sun, or hung on quickly constructed pole racks over a smudgy fire of good-tasting wood and smoked for a couple days. Even after smoking or sun drying for a couple of hours, the surface of the meat glazed over and it became easier to handle and transport than when fresh. This drying, of course, produced the original jerky.

Pemmican was made by pounding dried meat to a fine powder and mixing it about half and half by weight with rendered fat. This mixture was packed into rawhide bags, or lengths of cleaned intestine, where it would keep indefinitely. Because pemmican was so concentrated, compact, and supplied the native with almost all the nutrients his body needed (except for Vitamin C), it was and still is the most perfect food to carry on long journeys. When available, dried and pounded serviceberries or other fruits were added to the pemmican to provide the Vitamin C.

Innards

Intestines were very utilitarian. They could be sliced open, scraped clean, washed, cooked and eaten. Tubular sections were turned inside out, cleaned and, with the ends tied closed, used to store rendered fat, boiled brains, pemmican, and even to carry water. They were sometimes taken through the same process as buckskin—scraping, braining, softening and smoking—and then cut into long strips for strong cordage.

Because the deer's bladder is conveniently shaped and naturally waterproof, it was fashioned into a small pouch specifically intended to carry materials that must stay dry, especially tinder for firestarting, and the punky wooden bits for the hand-twirled fire drill.

Some Northern Paiute people of the Great Basin made interesting use of the deer's spleen as a poison for tipping arrows intended mostly for warfare. It supposedly took immediate effect, produced swelling and eventually death, but if used on game it did not affect the edibility of the meat. An old Paiute man from Surprise Valley described the process:

> "Our poison is made from the deer's akwatsi, black looking stuff on the intestine which looks like the liver but is smaller. Cook it in the ashes and let it dry. It smells bad. Stick the arrowpoint in and let it dry, or rub on the poison with the finger. There is no cure, so you have to be careful, especially if your finger is cut."

(It is probable that there is nothing inherently poisonous in the spleen, but that blood poisoning could easily stem from an arrow wound becoming infected. Other Paiute poisoning methods call for enticing a rattlesnake to bite a fresh liver or spleen, letting these ferment for a few days, then sticking the arrowpoints in the rotted meat.)

Several years ago, determined to make full use of a deer, I cooked up the spleen thinking it was part of the liver. My "spleen stew" tasted absolutely horrible, but I dutifully ate most of it, all the while telling myself only my own food prejudices made it taste so bad. I suffered no ill effects other than revulsion! Most unpleasant experiences tend to mellow with time in one's memory, but that stewed spleen just gets worse every time I think about it.

Antlers

Bone and antler probably provided more raw materials for manufactures than any other parts of the deer. They can be used similarly for many tools, but antler was better suited for some. It is softer, more elastic and resilient than bone, and has less tendency to crack and split.

Antler tines were first girdled with a sharp stone, then snapped into convenient lengths for use as pressure flakers in the manufacture of chipped stone scrapers, knives, drills and projectile points. Heavier sections of antler were used as billets for percussion stoneworking.

Along the coast, antler was cut and ground into wedges for splitting wood. Large antler tines functioned as crosspiece handles on hardwood root-digging sticks. Each tine had an inch-wide hole drilled laterally through its center so it could be slipped onto the top end of the digger to provide better leverage when the pointed stick was shoved into the ground next to a fat, juicy root. Sometimes the antler tines themselves were used to dig roots.

Sections of antler were commonly shaped into knife, scraper, and other handles, delicately incised and carved beads, figurines, decorative pendants, plus most of the uses made of bone as listed below. During the rutting season as an aid to hunting, whole antlers were clacked together by a concealed hunter to attract other deer.

Bone

Deer bones come in such a variety of dimensions that many tools and articles are already suggested by the natural forms, whether it be an unmodified longbone used as a fish-killing club or the tiny, smooth splinter-like bones from a deer's front feet that serve as preformed needles with only the drilling of eyes. With some incising here, some grinding there, some sanding and polishing, aboriginal man produced awls for basketry and skin working, pipes, beads of all sizes, ceremonial and game calling whistles, combs, points for arrows, spears and harpoons, drill bits, net gauges, weaving shuttles, mat creasers, simple to elaborate carved effigies, even snow goggles. The splinters of bone that remained after the marrow was extracted were shaped into needles, pins, dice and other gaming pieces, small awls, and many kinds of fishhooks.

Certain bones served especially well as specialized tools. The thin, flat scapula or shoulder blade was cut or broken to a jagged edge along one side and used to cut bunches of grasses for basketry, seed extraction, matting and thatching materials. Sometimes the deer's jawbone was similarly used, the teeth functioning as the cutting edge.

One end of the canon bone, the lowest longbone in a deer's front leg, was cut on a bevel, and tiny, sharp teeth were notched along the beveled edge. With a buckskin loop attached to the other end to brace the tanner's wrist, this tool was used with a downward stroking motion to remove any flesh, fat or connective tissue remaining on a hide.

The combination ulna and radius bones, also from the deer's foreleg, were used for the next step in tanning by the wet-scrape method. The long, thin edge of the ulna was ground sharp with abrasive stones and the naturally attached radius served as the handgrip. After the hide had been soaked in water long enough to slip the hair and loosen the epidermis, it was draped over a smooth section of log, and the ulna-radius tool was used like a drawknife to scrape off the unwanted material. Except for human skill and labor, the deer supplied all the necessary materials for tanning its own hide!

The myriad artifacts of deer and other bone, produced in aboriginal cultures, were defined by the tasks that needed to be accomplished and limited only by the imagination of the aboriginal mind. Archaeologists (perhaps limited, somewhat ironically, by their own imaginations) have excavated many obviously specialized bone and antler implements whose function in the native cultures still remains a mystery. I have barely touched on the known tools and their uses here.

The Aboriginal Ethic

Somewhere back in time—or perhaps ahead in time—on a crisp morning in the Moon of Plenty Harvest, a buckskin-clad figure crouches patiently in a chokecherry thicket above a well-used deer trail. The wind is right. His sinew-backed yew-wood bow is well greased with deer fat and curved taut by its tightly twisted deer sinew string. The arrow of oceanspray wood held lightly in his fingers is tipped with a black obsidian point he deftly flaked with the tip of a deer's antler and carefully bound to the shaft, like the three hawk feathers at the other end, with thread-thin sinew fibers first moistened in his mouth.

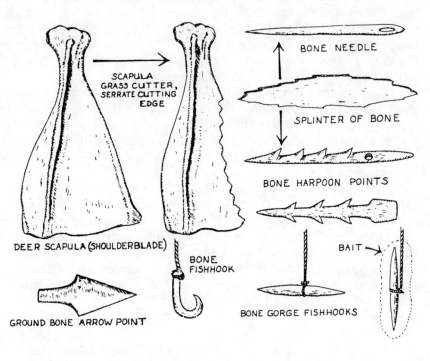

SCAPULA
GRASS CUTTER,
SERRATE CUTTING
EDGE

BONE NEEDLE

SPLINTER OF BONE

BONE HARPOON POINTS

DEER SCAPULA (SHOULDERBLADE)

BONE
FISHHOOK

BAIT

GROUND BONE ARROW POINT

BONE GORGE FISHHOOKS

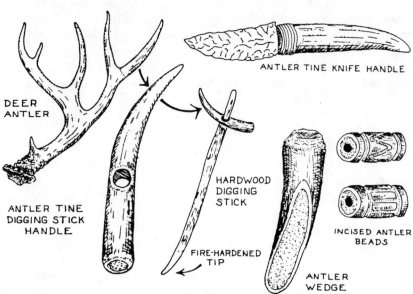

DEER
ANTLER

ANTLER TINE KNIFE HANDLE

HARDWOOD
DIGGING
STICK

ANTLER TINE
DIGGING STICK
HANDLE

FIRE-HARDENED
TIP

INCISED ANTLER
BEADS

ANTLER
WEDGE

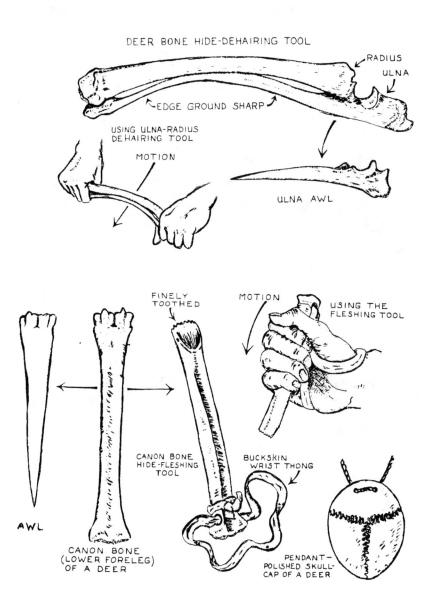

DEER BONE HIDE-DEHAIRING TOOL

RADIUS

ULNA

EDGE GROUND SHARP

USING ULNA-RADIUS DEHAIRING TOOL

MOTION

ULNA AWL

FINELY TOOTHED

MOTION

USING THE FLESHING TOOL

AWL

CANON BONE HIDE-FLESHING TOOL

BUCKSKIN WRIST THONG

CANON BONE (LOWER FORELEG) OF A DEER

PENDANT— POLISHED SKULL- CAP OF A DEER

Illustrations by Jim Riggs

Jim Riggs scraping membrane off a deer hide during a class at the Woodsmoke Rendezvous.

He has used the strength of the deer to fashion his tools so he may procure more deer. Through his ability to learn, the strength of the deer has become his own strength. It is alive inside him. He waits quietly while an unconcerned junco examines shriveled chokecherries among the branches above him. The deer will come; it always has.

Man has always been a hunter, a predator. As with all predators, the act of killing has been a necessary and integral part of living. But I believe there are moral and immoral approaches to killing. I believe any modern hunter can learn much from the beliefs and practices of the aboriginal man who lived closely with the earth. And perhaps he might find it rewarding to experiment with some of the aboriginal uses of the deer.

About midway through the course I came to the realization that I was not going to be taught by the common method of teaching, nor was I going to learn the things I came out expecting to learn. For example, the day when we found Tim. The wind was quite strong and I was quite tired, a combination that brought forth continual flows of foul, dirty words to relieve the frustrations at a situation over which I had no control. When I finally finished cooking in spite of the wind, Larry (Oog) called everyone together and told us a story of how the wind recorded everything that everyone said. A thousand hours of lecture couldn't have done a better job than that one story. I felt very small and ashamed of my immaturity but at the same time I was very glad that it had taken place because I realized that what I had done wasn't really necessary and it was only my own immaturity that made me do it.

Survival Student

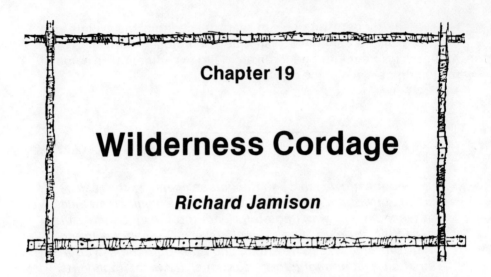

Chapter 19

Wilderness Cordage

Richard Jamison

The art of making rope or cordage from plants, leather, sinew or other fiberous material is called cording. It is one of man's earliest primitive skills. Primitive use of plant fiber is wide and includes not only cordage but blankets, sandals, baskets, clothing, bridles, nets for fishing and snares for capturing game. Because of the world we live in we have lost many of these skills, and have lost a part of our education in the process.

Remember the year of the Indianapolis 500 race when Parnelli Jones was the sure winner, only to lose from a breakdown caused by a $3 part?

Insignificant as it may seem, every small item is important in a survival situation. Either your bowstring works or it doesn't; either your trap springs or it doesn't.

Similarly can you imagine yourself dangling from a ledge by a piece of rope, your life dependent upon the strength of the line to which you are tied? Would you trust your life to hand-made cordage twined from so common a plant as milkweed or yucca?

Many primitive people of the past, as well as today, trust their very lives to rope made of plant fibers. Bridges are built over deep gorges and rapid rivers using the materials that nature offers. The Indian people who once populated the southwestern United States often used such rope in ascending their precarious dwellings, as well as to assist them in many chores related to their everyday living.

Under survival conditions there will be a time when you need some type of string or heavy cord.

I have noticed that the making of cordage from natural materials is overlooked in most survival books. Many authors are not familiar with, or knowledgeable in, primitive arts so therefore are not aware of the uses of the fiberous plants. This is unfortunate because the art of making cordage is not difficult to learn. But like any skill, it takes time and patience to do it well. I consider anyone a pro who has made 25 feet or more. If you balk at 25 feet, consider the fact that netting made by primitive people has been found to contain miles of cordage.

Gathering Materials

When looking for cordage plants, there are several things that should be considered. First, make sure the plant has a fiber. Second, be sure that the fiber is of an adequate length (short pieces of fiber are not as strong as the longer ones). Third, that the fiber has reasonable strength, and last that the plant is pliable.

Cordage should not be made from material that is not strong enough to do the job intended. For instance, useful cordage from the inner bark of the cottonwood tree would not be suitable for a bowstring.

Good materials that can be used in making cordage include dogbane, yucca, milkweed, stinging nettle, and sage, as well as the inner bark of trees such as the cottonwood, cedar and juniper. This inner bark is often abundant in large quantities in many areas and provides good material for weaving blankets, clothing and for bedding.

It is important to know the useful plants in all stages of growth so that you can recognize them readily when needed and when in their dry state.

Many plants fall into four categories. They are (1) edible, (2) poisonous (3) medicinal, and (4) used for plant construction. A large percentage of them fall into two or more categories. For instance, dogbane is a poisonous plant but is excellent in making cordage. The same is true of milkweed—it is considered an edible plant and can also be made into cordage. The yucca plant fits into three of the four categories—the fruit and flowers are edible, the dry stalks can be used as fire board and drill for fire by friction, the roots are medicinal and make an excellent soap substitute, the spines can be used as needle and thread for quick repair jobs and the fibers make a strong cordage.

Nettle can be found in moist areas in many parts of the country. It can be collected green but should then be dried to extract the fiber more easily and to eliminate shrinking of the completed cordage. Be very careful when collecting nettle, as the sting can be quite painful.

My favorite fiber plant is the dogbane. As I mentioned, it is considered poisonous but also contains one of the strongest fibers of the wild plants. Its reddish hue makes it easy to recognize during the fall and winter months when it is dry and ready to collect.

Yucca is unique in that it can be used while still green, when necessary, thus eliminating the time-consuming pounding and extracting process. The fiber of the yucca is found in the core of the stem opposed to the outer layer as with dogbane and milkweed. For a strong, fine-textured cordage it should be soaked for several days to loosen the fiber, then dried and gently pounded into silky threads. Several Indian tribes used this very fine fiber for weaving lovely cloth and baskets.

Milkweed also yields strong material for cordage, and its availability in areas where dogbane and the other plants are lacking makes it even more valuable. The milky juice within the plant makes it necessary to thoroughly dry it before beginning to extract the fiber. The dry seed pods which remain on the stem in the fall and winter make it easy to recognize in this stage.

The plants mentioned here grow in many geographical areas of the United States, but you may wish to test other species of plants native to your part of the country to find out if they are suitable for making cordage. Remember, your main concern is with strength, pliability and the length of the fiber.

Pound the stems until the fibers break loose and separate from the pith.

Extracting the Fibers

Most plant fiber is located on the outer part of the plant stem. In order to extract it, the inner pith must be separated from the fiber. While laying the stem on your leg or some smooth surface, use a gentle pounding motion with a rounded stick or smooth mallet. This will crack the stem without breaking the length of the fiber. At this point you can rub and roll the pulp from the remaining fiber by hand, again being careful not to break the length of the fibers. The result of this process is soft, flax-like threads which will be quite pliable.

Now that your material has been extracted from the plant, you are ready to begin the steps in making the cordage.

Technique

There are several methods of twisting the fiber, but the basic principle is preparing it by rolling the piece down your leg with your open palm until it is rounded and reasonably uniform in size. Now, taking the resulting string, bend it about two-thirds in half (in other words, leave one end one-third longer than the other). The small loop in the bend will be your starting point and should be held between the left thumb and forefinger if you are righthanded. You will have two loose ends hanging from the loop, taking the top piece between the thumb and forefingers on the left hand to hold the twist secure. Now fold the strand you have just twisted toward you, or counter-clockwise, and repeat the procedure with the opposite strand, the fingers on the left hand moving toward each new twist to hold it secure.

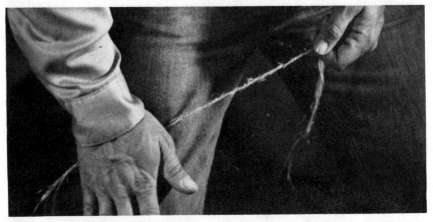

Roll the fibers on the thigh to remove the bark from the strands and to make the string more uniform.

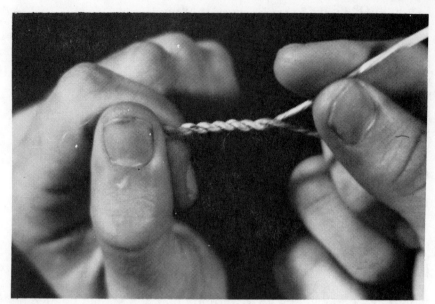

While holding the loop between the thumb and forefingers, twist the two ends counterclockwise.

Yucca cordage (top) and dogbane cordage (bottom).

When you reach approximately three inches from the end of your shortest strand, lay a new piece along the side, overlapping it to give a strong splice, and roll the two together. Continue the twisting and folding until the desired length is reached. Your cordage will not unravel due to the clockwise counter-clockwise twist which actually tightens itself.

The strength of your cord will depend upon the thickness of your strand. Two or three strands of cordage may be twisted together in this manner for more strength, as needed. Be sure that your splices are not at the same point, or opposite in your cordage, because this will weaken the strand. Also, try to make uniform strands to insure against weak spots.

Sinew Cordage

Sinew or animal tendon is the strongest natural material available and should be used in making such items as bowstrings, weapons and tools. Dried sinew must be prepared by pounding it until it is whitened and the fiber is separated. Be careful not to pound so vigorously that you break or cut the strands of fiber. After the sinew has been folded and twisted by the methods described for plant fiber, it is finished by stretching it between two points and rubbing saliva or other liquid into it until all the rough spots are smoothed out. It must then be allowed to dry in this position.

I have always found it rewarding to seek out the various plants and explore their many uses. Even my small children enjoy working with the plants and are quite apt at making cordage. It is surprising how quickly young children learn to identify the different species and their uses. It would be wonderful if we could instill this knowledge and appreciation at an early age so they could add upon it throughout their lives.

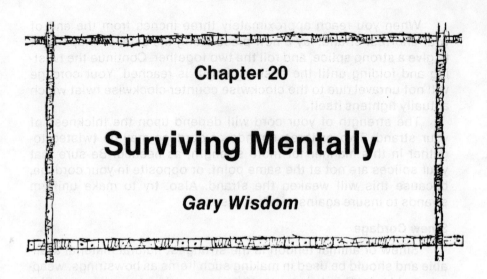

Chapter 20

Surviving Mentally

Gary Wisdom

When you find yourself in a survival situation there are several facts which you should remember. The most important fact is that the obstacles you have to overcome are not so much geographical and physical ones, but mental obstacles.

No matter how well prepared you are, you will probably never completely convince yourself that *it can happen to you.* But, as the records show, it can. So, you should understand what these psychological obstacles are before you start collecting survival facts and information.

Mental Obstacles

Mental obstacles all fall under the general heading of that very normal and common emotion called FEAR. Fear of the unknown, fear of discomfort, fear of your own weaknesses; and, in many cases, even though these other fears are overcome to some extent, a lack of confidence in their own fortitude and ability has broken people who could otherwise have fared much better.

Important areas of concern should be (1) how you react to various situations, (2) what feelings, expressions, and reactions in yourself mean, (3) your tolerance limits, (4) how to maintain, care for and effectively use your abilities in order to perform, resist, endure, and control yourself, and (5) how to apply helpful influence to your companions.

Physical Reactions

Nature has endowed you with biological reaction mechanisms which generally aid your adaption to stress. The bodily changes resulting from fear and anger, for example, tend to increase your alertness and provide you with extra energy. These same mechanisms, however, can betray you under survival conditions.

In a survival situation you will be exposed to certain common stresses. These are: fear and anxiety, pain, injury and illness, cold or heat, thirst, hunger, fatigue, sleep deprivation, boredom, loneliness and isolation. Each of these common physical stresses brings about a number of reactions which can be recognized and dealt with appropriately. The stresses that cause these reactions vary considerably, and specific ways of reacting vary among individuals. You should also be aware that these stresses often occur at the same time. Anticipating them can be a valuable tool in coping with them.

But tools and training are not enough, and neither of them are effective without the "will to survive." Cultivate good survival attitudes. Keep your mind on your main goal and keep everything else in perspective.

Emotional States

Already mentioned are the common stresses of survival. There are also some associated emotional states which must be understood just as survival equipment and conditions are understood. In the survival situation the most important elements in the determination of success or failure are (1) yourself, and (2) your companions, if any.

Two of the gravest general dangers to survival are concessions to comfort and having a passive outlook. These dangers must be recognized because of their general implications and their relation to the specific survival stresses. Both dangers represent attitudes which follow lines of least resistance, and overrule your effort or desire to cope with stress. Both dangers represent attitudes of primary concern with the immediate situation rather than the overall problems of survival. To survive successfully, you must be able to master both of these tendencies. Reason is the key to this change of attitude—reason which identifies discomfort as a temporary problem in comparison with the tremendous advantage of endurance.

Survival Training

Survival training is like life insurance—you never need it until you need it. How convenient it would be if you could just skip your life insurance premiums until the month before you die; obviously it doesn't work that way.

Perhaps comparing life insurance to survival training is mis-leading. Life insurance doesn't guarantee that you will live longer, while survival training does. Survival training is the only real form of life insurance . . . and the odds are that you *will* be around to collect on the policy.

Chapter 21

Basics of Keeping Warm

Richard Jamison

My job is not to lessen the misery, but to teach the student what to expect and how to deal with it.

It was July in the desert of Southern Utah. I was running a trip with fifteen students, and had gone into the area a few days early to look over the country with one of my instructors.

The days were hot and the nights just right. I had my sleeping bag with me and a foam pad, but this time of the year was just right for sleeping on top of the pad with just a light jacket.

As I lay there, secure and warm, my thoughts went back to some of the times when I wasn't so comfortable; in fact, times that I was downright miserable. Like when I was on the move and tired, got a fire started and flopped down beside it with aching muscles, only to be awakened at 2 a.m. in a downpour of rain.

With these thoughts, I dropped off to sleep, and the following morning prepared to pick up my charges for the next ten days. These were people who, for the most part, had never slept without the comfort of a sleeping bag. This was a new day, a new experience for the students, several nights not to be forgotten and, I hoped, lessons well learned.

As we got our gear together, I couldn't help notice the difference in their blankets. I saw everything from large quilts to sheet-thin blankets that were too short to cover a student's feet and still keep his shoulders warm. I silently sympathized because I have personally been stuck with a blanket that was too short and it does make a difference.

After much seemingly needless shuffle for the amount of gear we were taking in (extra socks, shirt and jacket) the donut rolls were tied and tossed over the shoulders of the soon-to-be cave dwellers and we were off. The students learn that a blanket is not only for keeping warm, it also serves to carry all their belongings for the for the expedition. I used to do some backpacking, but found myself always looking for items to fill all the pockets whether I needed it or not. This kind of traveling can really spoil you.

Campsite Selection is Important

After walking most of the day, we were more than ready to find shelter. We located our camp with water nearby, but not so close that we would be bothered by insects. Camping near water is much colder than locating higher, so we situated ourselves on the eastern-facing slope to take advantage of the warmth of the morning sun. We remarked, too, that the cool breezes blow down the valleys at night, causing a temperature variance of up to 20 degrees in lower areas.

Wear Adequate Clothing

To avoid the obvious problems we always tell our students to wear a cotton long-sleeved shirt, a wool sweater or shirt and a light-weight but warm jacket. There is a specific reason for this combination relative to keeping warm. Cotton keeps the wool and resulting itching away from the skin, and acts as an additional layer of insulation as well as protecting arms from the sun during the afternoon. Wool, of course, is the best source of warmth available because it has unique ability to remain warm even when wet. The outer jacket offers another layer of insulation that can be shed or worn as needed to regulate the body thermostat. I might add that wool gloves, hat, socks and pants are all valuable additions to your outdoor wardrobe.

Ideally I like to have the students gather wood early in the afternoon to avoid stumbling around in the dark, but also because the students tend to put all their clothing on in the evening chill, then work up a sweat dragging in a wood supply. The resulting perspiration will cause chilling, which is hard to overcome in the night air.

On a survival trip you soon learn to sleep with all your available clothing on, including your boots for maximum insulation. Caution should be used, however, not to sleep with your feet too close to the fire. Believe it or not, soles have been burned right off the bottom of boots without the wearers knowledge. Hair can also easily catch on fire if your head is too near the fire, so the best and safest way to sleep is lengthwise of the fire.

Utilize Sleeping Fires

When utilizing fires for keeping warm, you must take into consideration the types of fires to be used. With fifteen students on the trail, three long fires can be used with people sleeping lengthwise and the soft night breezes will move the warm air to your advantage and everyone can share in the maintenance of the fire.

This student takes advantage of a long trench fire and uses cattail leaves beneath him for insulation.

Wood gathering itself takes a little getting used to if you are accustomed to a sleeping bag and tent, but it makes all the difference when you are trying to keep warm with just a blanket or your jacket.

Long, medium-sized logs are the best suited for this type of firebed, as they can be shoved in as they burn on one end. This also saves time and effort of gathering kindling which burns up much too fast for sleeping fires. Besides, most people try to break it up with their feet, which could lead to serious problems, such as sprained ankles, broken bones or eye injuries from flying particles of wood.

The first night is always the worst for most students, probably because they don't know what to expect. Most of them wake up several times during the night. I can almost set my watch by it, and this was no exception. About 2 a.m. I heard some rustling and one of the younger students softly crying. I quickly perceived the problem. She was sleeping about 5 feet from her fire, had placed her wood pile too far to reach and was using her wool sweater for a pillow. After correcting these factors, she was able to sleep well for the remainder of the night.

Gather Plenty of Insulation

A good layer of insulation beneath you is just as important to keeping warm as the covering on top. Approximately 70 percent of heat loss is downward. If the ground is damp from rain or other moisture, you are going to spend a miserable night even with a good fire. Insulation was gathered by shredding dry bark from cottonwood trees, cedar, juniper and sage. Also cattail down and dry grass were available in sufficient abundance to be useful.

For my own survival comfort I often sew a piece of cotton backing on one side of my wool blanket with pockets and a closing flap. Insulative material can be inserted for more warmth, then removed for less bulk in moving cross country, or when warmer weather lessens the need.

Use Rocks to Reflect Heat

The third day found us near some overhangs which we utilized as a reflector as we slept beneath the shelter of the cliffs. I might mention that it is imperative that you understand where to build your sleeping fires when using rocks for a heat reflector. Under no circumstances should you build your fire beneath the overhang. The heat from the fire and possible moisture accumulated in cracks of the rocks will expand and cause the entire ledge to break off and crash down as you sleep. The fires should be built outside the shelter area and the heat will relect off the cave walls to toast you on both sides. Other materials can be stacked in such a manner as to act as a heat reflector if natural formations are not available.

Huddle for Warmth

On the tenth and last night we encountered some rain starting early in the day. Since the two most important factors in keeping warm are staying dry and keeping out of the wind chill, we made an effort to secure our shelters against wind and rain. The chill factor cut through like a knife, so we built up our fires and took turns

Build your fire outside the shelter area and reflect heat off the rock wall, and sleep between the fire and the wall.

sleeping and keeping the fires going. A good bed of coals will burn right through a storm if it is fed regularly, and can be a real lifesaver in drying out damp clothes and bedding.

In an effort to keep warm we slept together in twos and threes. Three people would spread one blanket on the ground and cuddle together under two covers to take better advantage of the available body heat.

Hitting the trail with only a blanket, as we do, may not be the ideal situation, but it is done for a reason. It teaches the student self-confidence in his ability to keep warm, and is one of the best lessons that can be learned in the field.

Index

If you walked into the woods today, what
would the deer and the coyote smell . . . rubber,
exhaust fumes, and asphalt?

Stand In The Woodsmoke For Awhile

A woodsman knows the value of *Woodsmoke.*
It puts him in tune with the wilds and
takes away the fumes of civilization.

If you have enjoyed *The Best of Woodsmoke,* you really should
set your courses for those future columns rising on the horizon. The
spark has been struck, and the flames are ready to warm you from
now on.

You can sit with *Woodsmoke* and feel the lore of the trail and
the security of the homestead hearth. The skills for living will keep
your fingers busy around the evening fire wherever you are. *Woodsmoke* will be sizzling with hump roast and ashcakes; stoneage
skills and homespun hints for a better and more enduring life style;
adventure and history along with a few tall tales now and then.

Woodsmoke aims to help you build confidence and a sense of
adventure in yourself by putting you in touch with newer and better
ways to become one with nature and with society. Contrary to the
pessimistic opinions of some people, *Woodsmoke* believes that
man is the master of his destiny, and that he truly is a part of this
wonderful universe.

Lie down just outside the fire's dim light, and gaze at the limitless sky; feel the stillness of the land and let the fresh breezes bathe
you in your own *Woodsmoke* . . . and while you're at it, invite your
friends to join you—let *Woodsmoke* blow in their direction, too.

. . . .

WOODSMOKE JOURNAL
P.O. Box 474
Centerville, Utah 84014

Send me a 6-issue subscription of Woodsmoke Journal for only $8.00.
My check or money order is enclosed. Outside U.S. add $10.00.

Please check appropriate box: ☐ New subscription ☐ Renewal
☐ Send information on workshops and expeditions.

_____

Name

_____

Address   City   State   Zip